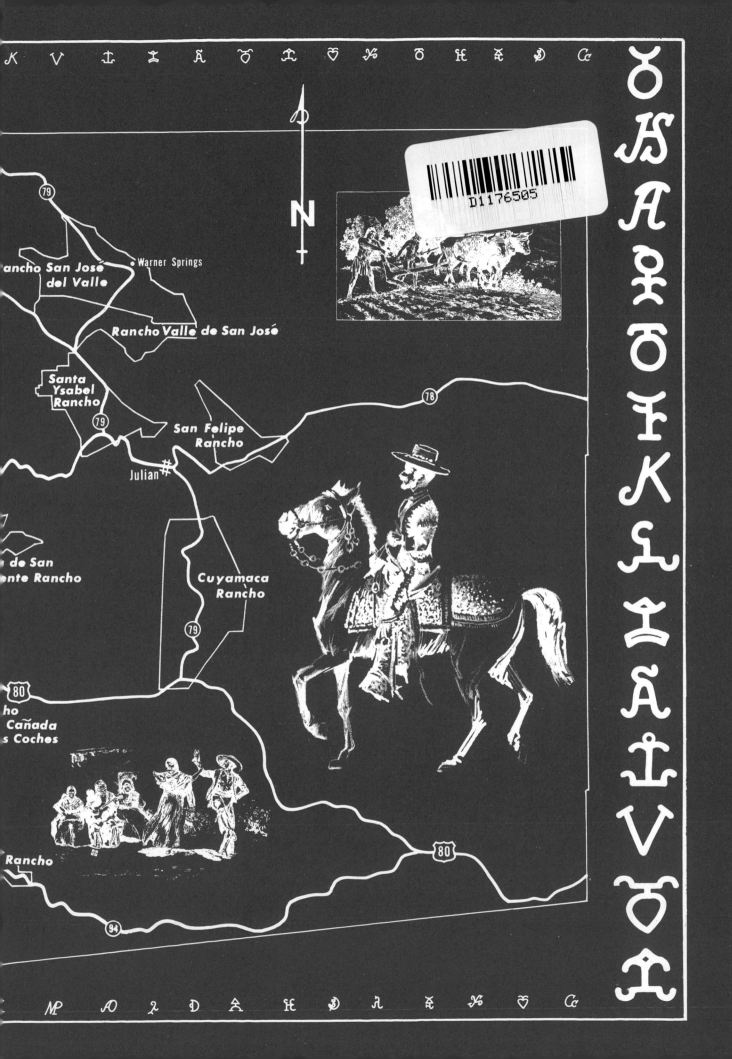

Rancho San José
del Valle

Warner Springs

Rancho Valle de San José

Santa
Ysabel
Rancho

San Felipe
Rancho

Julian

de San
ente Rancho

Cuyamaca
Rancho

ho
Cañada
s Coches

Rancho

Historic Ranchos of San Diego

COVER ILLUSTRATION

A gay wedding party, with the bride on her wedding saddle, winds up the hill from the Santa Margarita Rancho, singing or playing musical instruments.

HISTORIC RANCHOS
OF SAN DIEGO

A COPLEY BOOK

Commissioned by JAMES S. COPLEY

Text by CECIL C. MOYER

Edited by RICHARD F. POURADE

PUBLISHED BY UNION-TRIBUNE PUBLISHING CO.

Dedication

In these modern times of rapid communication and transportation it is pleasing to reflect upon the pastoral scene of California in the early 19th century when neighbors only visited occasionally and often traveled more than a day to see each other.

Each rancho was a community within itself, far removed from central government and under the autocratic control of the ranchero to whom the vast tract of land had been granted.

Residents or visitors to San Diego County who today enjoy the comforts of the new era, in mind's fancy, may look back through the pages of this book to the serenity and romance of the days of the ranchos and learn which of the historic land grants they can associate with current situations or residence.

It is hoped *Historic Ranchos of San Diego* will bring pleasant reflections from a picturesque and romantic era never again to be seen in our world.

JAMES S. COPLEY

Contents

Foreigners merged with Californios in Days of the Dons. In English hunting coat, Edward Stokes at Warner's Pass agrees to carry plea for troops to San Diego for Gen. Stephen Watts Kearny during Mexican War.

Introduction

The literature of the great rancho period of California is steeped in romanticism. The period is defined generally as the time between the breakup of the Franciscan mission system and the Americanization of California that came with the end of the United States-Mexican War.

In San Diego, the rancho period began later than in some other areas of the state, all of its ranchos having been granted during the time California was a province of Mexico. But the period lasted longer in that change came slower and ranching remained a way of life well into the late 1800's.

The rancho period, so romantically known as the Days of the Dons, actually had two phases. Together they covered less than thirty years. But it was a feudal-like era in which each man was king and governmental restraints were nonexistent, or limited.

Even under Spanish rule, California was a remote territory subject to little direct influence of the King or the Church. The revolution in Mexico brought independence to a new nation, and to California a further lessening of the always fragile ties of domination from Mexico City.

California was open to intrusions from all directions. When the Mexican revolutionists decreed the secularization of the missions, vast tracts of land in California were made available to soldiers and settlers, as well as to American traders and adventurers who had felt, or hoped, that someday California would fall into their hands.

Lands were passed out lavishly to the faithful. Tremendous herds of cattle provided hides for shoe manufacturers in New England and for tallow to be made into soap for South America. Within fifteen years, however, the more foresighted Dons saw that it could not last forever, that as the motherland of Mexico held little control over their affairs and their lands, and could provide little or no military protection, California might soon have to become a country of its own or become a possession of England, or of some other foreign nation.

The government in Washington knew that too. The war between the United States and Mexico perhaps merely hastened the inevitable. The resistance of the Californios was limited. California became a part of the United States.

In the unsettled times that followed, the hapless Dons awoke to the fact that, despite pledges, the titles to the lands they had obtained through what they believed had been legal means, or by thinly disguised seizures, had to be justified before a United States Land Commission, and often again in the courts. Hard times followed.

Soon afterward the discovery of gold brought new life to the ranchos of the south. Great herds of cattle were driven north to Sacramento and San Francisco. For a time the silver on saddles grew heavier and lands larger. But that period, too, passed and the Days of the Dons were numbered. Few of them were able to hold onto their ranchos. The pressures of law suits and heavy migrations of land-hungry Americans brought about a new era of agriculture and towns more than of ranching.

Though ownerships changed, many of the more remote ranchos persisted through the years, shrinking or increasing in size from time to time. Today on many of the original rancho lands cattle still roam the hills and valleys as they did a hundred years ago.

But the life of the ranchos, or the Days of the Dons, lived in memory. This is the story of how the ranchos came about, and what happened to them, and if it too breathes with nostalgia, you can say that California does that to all of us, no matter when we came to its golden shore.

RICHARD F. POURADE

With crude maps often enlivened with color, the Dons pressed their claims to ranchos granted by Mexico. José Joaquín Ortega's diseño *outlined Rancho Santa María which in time became site of town of Ramona.*

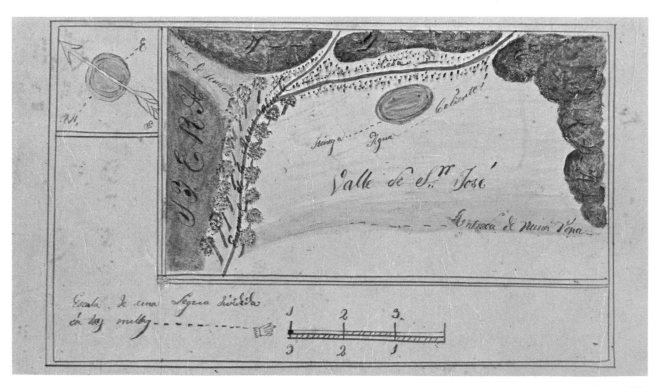

Hand-drawn diseño, *submitted by J. J. Warner to support his court claim for Rancho Valle de San José. The northern part of the rancho was known as Rancho San José del Valle. The two became Warner Ranch.*

1

Los Peñasquitos Rancho

Most of San Diego County's huge Mexican land grants were awarded to friends or relatives of the various governors who ruled California between 1823 and 1846. Three ranchos, for reasons history does not explain, were given to Indians, and two went to military men for "meritorious service."

Capt. Francisco María Ruiz, *comandante* of the Presidio of San Diego, was one of the latter and he was awarded the first grant in the county. The year was 1823, the governor was Luis Antonio Arguello, and the grant was for an 8,486-acre tract known as Los Peñasquitos Rancho.

Los Peñasquitos means "the little cliffs" and is pronounced pen-yas-kee'-tos. As might be expected, such a tract only twenty miles north of San Diego changed considerably in more than a century—yet as late as 1968 cattle still grazed the rolling hills and grassy valleys.

Los Peñasquitos Rancho played an interesting part in San Diego County's history. After the Battle of San Pasqual, December 6, 1846, in which the Californios, including some of the Dons of the county's ranchos, attacked Gen. Stephen Watts Kearny's troops, the tattered American survivors moved slowly toward San Diego. The evening of December 11 the soldiers reached Los Peñasquitos, where they were welcomed and given food. The following day

they moved down Soledad Canyon and on to San Diego.

Captain Ruiz, the first owner of the rancho, was born in 1754 in Loreto, Baja California. At the age of twenty-six he enlisted in the army and soon after was sent to California. He was a sergeant at Santa Barbara, became a lieutenant in 1805, then was transferred to San Diego, where in 1820 he was made a captain. He soon became *comandante* of the San Diego garrison and remained in that post until his retirement in 1827 at the age of seventy-three.

Ruiz had never married, and spent most of his time after his retirement at his home in San Diego, making only periodic journeys to Los Peñasquitos. Records do not disclose the extent of his ranching activities, but he did raise cattle on the rancho and constructed a large adobe house, of which only crumbling walls remained in the 1960's.

On March 15, 1837, Captain Ruiz appeared before the *alcalde*, or mayor, of San Diego and transferred ownership of the rancho to Don Francisco María Alvarado, an Old Town resident who had cared for him in his declining years. Ruiz died in 1839 at the age of eighty-five.

Don Francisco had long been prominent in San Diego affairs. In 1837 he was a *regidor*, or councilman; in 1840-41 he was town treasurer, and he became a justice of the peace in 1845. After the death

Crumbling adobe walls were all that remained in 1968 of the once beautiful home of Don Francisco María Alvarado on Los Peñasquitos Rancho. Don Francisco inherited the rancho from Capt. Francisco María Ruiz.

J. S. Taylor purchased Los Peñasquitos Rancho in 1883, constructed this adobe-and-wood ranchhouse and planted lemon trees. The trees soon succumbed to the winter cold. The house was in good repair in 1968.

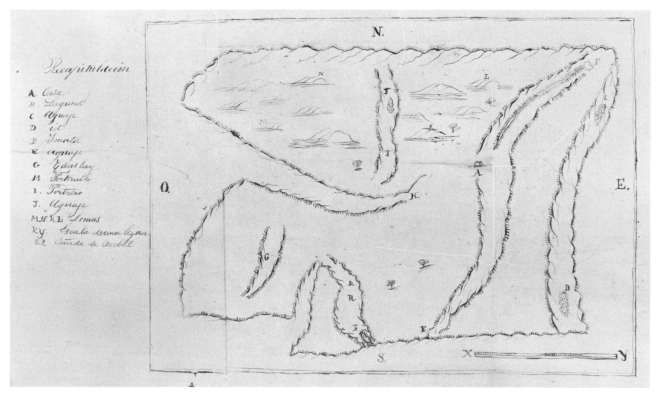

This is the way Don Francisco María Alvarado drew the map of Los Peñasquitos Rancho to prove his claim to the property before the U.S. Land Commission. Later purchases almost doubled the size of the rancho.

of Captain Ruiz, Alvarado spent most of his time at the rancho.

Pío Pico, who was governor of California briefly in 1832, and in 1845-46, and who owned Jamul Rancho, took possession of Los Peñasquitos through a sheriff's sale because of a $420 unpaid debt. But he soon returned the property to Don Francisco, to whom he was related.

By the time a patent to the land was granted in 1876, ownership had passed to Capt. George A. Johnson of the Colorado River Navigation Co., through his marriage to Don Francisco's daughter, Tomasa. Johnson was at one time a member of the state Legislature.

In 1881 the rancho was purchased for $35,000 by A. N. Lancaster, who sold it two years later to J. S. Taylor. The latter shipped in Durham cattle from Colorado to improve the quality of stock on the rancho. He also planted lemon trees, but the winter cold soon killed them.

Taylor constructed a new ranchhouse, a large U-shaped structure built of wood and adobe. This house was kept in good condition through the years.

Later owners of the rancho included Adolph Levi, pioneer San Diego business man, Charles F. Mohnike and Wirt Bowman, and finally the Sawday-Sexson interests.

A third ranchhouse was built about 1900 a half-mile east of the Taylor house. It was constructed of adobe and became the home of Mr. and Mrs. Russell Peavey, who modernized and rebuilt part of the structure.

The hills and valleys changed little through the years. In 1968 cowboys were still driving white-faced Herefords to holding corrals at the home ranch, and it didn't take much stretch of the imagination to visualize the hard-riding *vaqueros* and wild, horned cattle that ranged Los Peñasquitos a century before.

But change and progress are inevitable. Cities spread out to engulf many of the historic ranchos, and suburbs and shopping centers replace the once fenceless cattle ranges.

Through the years the rancho grew in size as

various owners purchased adjoining lands. The acreage totaled 14,000 before the population growth of San Diego County caused suburban expansion to encroach on the rancho.

In 1962, Sawday & Sexson, Inc., sold the property for home, business and recreational development. Both George Sawday, pioneer cattleman, and Oliver Sexson, once San Diego County under-sheriff, were deceased, and the corporation consisted of Mrs. George Sawday, president; Orville Cumming, secretary, and Mrs. Cumming, and Mr. and Mrs. Peavey.

One cannot but regret the passing of the Days of the Dons, when life was harder, but also more simple.

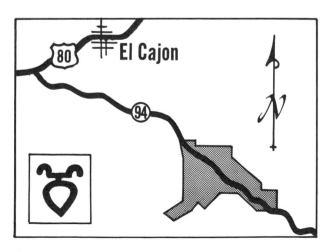

2

Jamul Rancho

Jamul Rancho has a colorful—and violent—past.

Its 8,926 acres were granted to Pío Pico, last Mexican governor of California, in 1829 by Gov. José María Echeandía, and the title was confirmed in 1831.

One hundred thirty-seven years later, Jamul Rancho, about twenty-five miles southeast of San Diego on Highway 94, comprised about 10,000 acres. It was still a cattle ranch, but, unlike the Dons of a century ago, its modern-day owners farmed also, growing Sudan grass, alfalfa and barley. Jamul is an Indian word meaning "slimy water" and is pronounced hah-mool.

Pío Pico and his brother, Andrés, were politically prominent in San Diego in the early 1800's. In 1832, Don Pío became governor for a period of twenty days, being replaced by Echeandía, and was again named governor in the closing months of Mexican rule, 1845-1846. In 1841 the Pico brothers were granted the huge Rancho Santa Margarita y las Flores, now the U. S. Marine Corps' Camp Pendleton.

Don Pío began stocking Jamul Rancho with cattle and horses as soon as he received the grant. He also constructed an adobe ranchhouse several hundred feet west of the junction of Jamul Creek and Dulzura Creek at the base of Jamul Mountain and

J. S. Harvey planted this orange and lemon orchard in Jamul Valley, although he never was the owner of Jamul Rancho. No trace remained in 1968 of the orchard; presumably the winter cold killed all the trees.

not far from the later-day Camp Minnewawa Forestry Station.

Don Andrés Pico, who later became a general in the Mexican forces, was in charge of the ranch from 1836 to 1838.

In 1837 the rancho was the the scene of an Indian raid and the kidnapping of two girls, which caused great excitement in San Diego when the news reached the little town.

Many of the San Diego area Indians had rebelled against the encroachment of the whites on what they considered to be their lands, and backed by the warlike Yuma tribes, plotted to exterminate the rancheros and even to attack San Diego. One of their first armed assaults was on Jamul Rancho.

Neither of the Pico brothers was at the rancho on that day in April when an Indian servant woman named Cesarea warned Doña Eustaquia López, widowed mother of the Picos, that a war party would soon attack the rancho.

The rancho *mayordomo*, Juan Leiva, assured Doña Eustaquia there was no danger as he and his *vaqueros* were well armed and prepared to fight.

Doña Eustaquia, however, did not share the rancho manager's confidence. With her three unmarried daughters, Feliciana, Jacinta and Ysidora, she fled in an ox-drawn *carreta* to nearby Jamacha Rancho and then on to San Diego.

Richard F. Pourade vividly described the attack in his book, *The Silver Dons*.

The night after the flight of the four women all was quiet at the rancho and the *mayordomo* and his men began to think the attack plot was just a figment of the Indian woman's imagination.

Don Pío Pico built this house on Jamul Rancho after Indians burned the original ranchhouse in 1837. The Daley family remodeled and enlarged the house, retaining the charm of the early-day Mexican architecture.

It was the following evening when a large force of Indians, some on horseback, attacked the rancho. Several *vaqueros* were killed in the first onslaught and Leiva was badly wounded. His son, Antonio, was among those killed. Leiva staggered to the room where the guns were kept just in time to see an Indian servant woman lock the door and then run. Leiva fought bravely but was finally killed by the Indians.

The attackers threatened to kill Leiva's wife, Doña María, and small son, Claro, but finally freed them after stripping them of their clothing. The two walked the entire distance to Mission San Diego; Doña María died a short time later.

The Indians tied Leiva's two daughters, Tomasa, age fifteen, and Ramona, twelve, on horses, then set fire to the ranchhouse. They rounded up all the horses and cattle they could find and fled in the direction of the Colorado River.

The two girls were never rescued. A military expedition commanded by Sgt. Macedonio González, an uncle of the girls, tracked the Indian war party into the mountains. The troopers finally caught up with the Indians and reported sighting the two sisters atop a rocky hill. González said the captives' bodies were smeared with white paint and their hair had been cut in Indian fashion. The soldiers killed some of the Indians but the main band escaped with the girls.

The rescue expedition was on the trail nearly four months and while the troopers had numerous encounters with the Indians and killed many of them, the girls were never seen again. Years later it was reported they had been taken as wives by Indian chiefs.

The Picos did not rebuild the ranchhouse after the fire. They did, however, construct another and larger adobe house about two miles away. This struc-

6

Pio Pico, twice governor of California, was given the 8,926-acre Jamul Rancho as a land grant in 1829.

Little remains of the original Pico ranchhouse. The ravages of time and vandals have taken their toll. A few chunks of the original stone foundation were still visible in 1968, but the adobe walls had disappeared. There was the stump of a huge palm tree nearby and the area around where the house stood was dotted with holes dug by seekers of a treasure that legend said was buried by a gang of bandits that used the ruins of the ranchhouse for a hideout.

ture, after several remodelings, became the modern home of Lawrence Daley, his wife and son George.

The Miguel de Pedrorena family succeeded the Picos as the next owner of Jamul Rancho. In the late 1800's squatters occupied choice parts of the rancho and several of them were lynched by rancheros.

John D. Spreckels, San Diego financier, was the next owner. In 1915 he sold the rancho to Louis J. Wilde, mayor of San Diego, for a reported $300,000. Baron Long, owner of the U. S. Grant Hotel, and several partners then bought the property.

George R. Daley, a road contractor, purchased the rancho in 1927. He made many improvements, including some remodeling of the Pico ranchhouse, and also added to the acreage.

After his death, his nephews, Lawrence and Donald, took over the rancho. Lawrence remodeled and added to the old ranchhouse without destroying the charm of the early California architecture.

3

Otay Rancho and Janal Rancho

Janal and Otay were adjoining ranchos granted in 1829 to a brother and sister of the prominent Estudillo family.

Don José Antonio Estudillo, who built Casa de Estudillo, later better known as Ramona's Marriage Place in Old Town, received the 4,436-acre Janal Rancho by grant from Gov. José María Echeandía; Doña Magdalena Estudillo was given Otay Rancho, which totaled 6,657 acres.

Janal is pronounced hah-nal' and is an Indian word meaning "spongy ground." Otay is pronounced o-tie; it is an Indian word and means "brushy."

Don José had held several official positions in early-day San Diego, including *alcalde, juez de paz,* or justice of the peace, and later, county treasurer and assessor. He had eight children.

That Janal and Otay ranchos were jointly operated for many years, although their cattle carried different brands, is indicated by the fact that many old maps mark both with the name Otay. Later maps marked Janal with the name Otay Domínguez, and still later ones carried only the name Janal.

Don José was married to Doña María Victoria, daughter of Don Cristobal Domínguez, grantee of the large San Pedro Rancho near Los Angeles, but there was nothing to indicate Don Cristobal had any financial interest in the Janal.

Many of the rancheros a century ago had difficulty proving their rights to the huge land grants given by the lavish hands of Mexican governors before the American conquest of California. Richard F. Pourade in his book *The Silver Dons,* tells of their difficulties:

"The grand Don of San Diego, José Antonio Estudillo, died in 1852 at the age of forty-seven. With him passed much of the Spanish flavor that had lingered ever since the revolution in Mexico. The grace and ease of the pastoral days were gone. His home had been a fortress in time of trouble and its chapel had kept flickering the flame of Catholic faith.

"He and his family held the adjoining ranchos of Janal and Otay, and his son, José G. Estudillo, went before the United States Land Commission, as did all the Dons, to fight for the lands granted to them which they thought had been guaranteed by the American invaders. The Land Act of 1851 made it necessary for all claimants to present their petitions for verification within two years or forfeit their

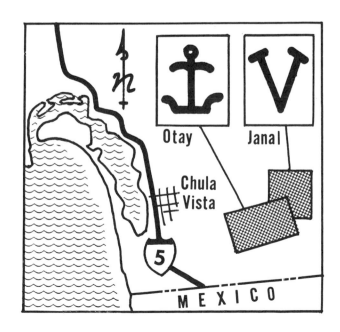

Trees hide the spacious house and grounds of Rancho del Otay, once a part of Janal Rancho, but later incorporated into the huge Otay Rancho. Original house was constructed as a hunting lodge by John D. Spreckels.

rights, and as the burden of proof was placed on the Dons, they often were hard-pressed to locate the carelessly drawn titles and maps of by-gone days. Friends testified for each other as to boundaries that were both vague and altered by use and claims of squatters. The Land Commission hearings went on for ten years, and court hearings followed upon them, until lawyer fees and court costs had eaten up much of the wealth that the land had represented."

Don José Guadalupe Estudillo received a U.S. patent to the Janal grant in 1872, and in the same year his aunt, Doña Magdalena, received a patent to Otay Rancho.

In another of Pourade's book series, *The Glory Years*, the historian tells of an early-day stage route across the Otay and Janal grants:

"The first San Diego-Yuma route to run all within United States territory was laid out by the county surveyor, James Pascoe, early in 1869. It was twenty-five miles shorter than the old wagon trail through Warner's Pass to Yuma, and it had fifty-five miles less of desert travel.

"Pascoe's route turned up the Otay River course at La Punta, thirteen miles south of San Diego. It followed the river to the Otay Lake basin, passing through Otay, Janal and Jamul ranchos, then traced the course of Dulzura Creek easterly through the valleys, climbing into the summit country of San Diego's eastern mountain barrier along the course followed by the present State Route 94 through Potrero and Campo. It crossed the high rolling country by way of Milquatay Valley, twelve miles

José Guadalupe Estudillo inherited Janal Rancho from his father. His aunt was given Otay Rancho.

from Campo to Jacumba, then passed ten miles from Jacumba eastward and down the steep grade at Mountain Springs. It was eighty-six miles from San Diego to the head of the desert. From there it was 110 miles across the desert to Yuma."

No evidence remains of any early-day ranch-house on either the Janal or Otay. Both ranches changed hands several times during the years and the boundaries of both were altered as parcels of land were bought or sold.

The Janal lost its original identity and much of its size; its remaining acreage in 1968 totaled about

3,500, its cattle were gone and its rolling hills and valleys were devoted to growing of barley. It became the Fenton Ranch and was owned by Emily Fenton Hunte, wife of Rear Adm. Louis H. Hunte, USN, retired.

Otay Rancho became Otay Ranch and its acreage grew to 20,000. About 500 cattle—polled Herefords, Black Angus and Santa Gertrudis—grazed on the rancho lands, and they carried the same brand used by Doña Magdalena Estudillo more than a century ago.

Otay Ranch was owned by United Enterprises, Inc., a family corporation consisting of the heirs of Stephen Birch, a New Jersey capitalist who bought the ranch in 1936. Birch's daughter, Mary, was the wife of Patrick R. Patrick, a former wing commander in the Royal Air Force. The Patricks resided at Rancho del Otay, once a part of the Janal grant but later included in the Otay holdings.

In September of 1968, 3,150 acres of the ranch were sold to John Quinn, a Los Angeles oil man, and Albert Gersten, head of the Gersten Construction Company of Los Angeles, for $5,292,500. The area, nearly surrounded by the city of Chula Vista, was to be used for home development and light industry.

All of the land for Upper Otay Reservoir and most of Lower Otay, owned by the city of San Diego, were taken from within the original boundaries of Janal Rancho.

The Patrick home, surrounded by trees, on a hill overlooking Upper Otay Reservoir, first was constructed as a hunting lodge by John D. Spreckels, who for a time, with E. S. Babcock and other financiers, controlled both Janal and Otay ranchos.

4

Rancho San José del Valle and Rancho Valle de San José

Jonathan Trumbull Warner was a Connecticut Yankee who became a Mexican Don and ruled one of the best and largest ranchos in San Diego County.

In 1968 cattle still roamed his empire of 44,322 acres, where cowboys roped and branded as the *vaqueros* did more than a century before. But there was a modern touch—a guest ranch that occupied the area where an Indian ranchería once stood. And the hot mineral springs which warmed the Indians on cold winter nights furnished water for swimming pools and a golf course.

Jonathan Warner migrated westward at the age of twenty-three with a fur-trading party. He arrived in California in November, 1831, and followed the immigrant trail through what is now Warner Ranch.

This beautiful valley had no significance for him then, for Los Angeles was his destination. He hunted otter for a time, then worked in a store owned by Don Abel Stearns. He learned to speak Spanish and made many Mexican friends, among them Don Pío Pico, twice governor of California.

In Pico's home he met Anita Gale, daughter of an English sea captain, who had been left as a ward with Pico's widowed mother, Doña Eustaquia. He

became a Mexican citizen, taking the name Juan José Warner, and married Miss Gale in 1837 at San Luis Rey Mission.

Before secularization of the missions the padres of both San Diego and San Luis Rey missions grazed their herds and flocks on the lands they called Valle de San José. There were many Indian rancherías in the valley, the largest one at Agua Caliente, later to become Warner Springs.

Silvestre de la Portilla received a grant for part of the valley in 1836. Boundaries were not clearly defined, and in 1840 José Antonio Pico, brother of Andrés and Pío Pico, applied for and received a grant for the area called Agua Caliente. This became Rancho San José del Valle, totaling 26,688 acres. Portilla's grant of 17,634 acres, to the south, was called Rancho Valle de San José.

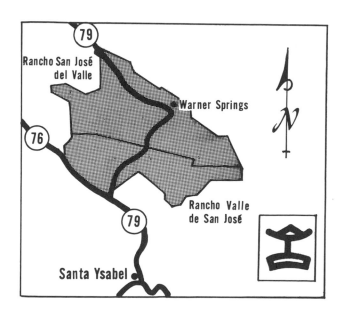

Both Pico and Portilla, however, soon abandoned their ranchos because of continuing troubles with the Indians. In 1844, Warner, citing the fact that both ranchos had been abandoned, applied for and received a grant to the entire valley.

Warner built an adobe house and trading post four miles south of Agua Caliente. He made no at-

Silvestre de la Portilla drew this diseño, or map, *to show boundaries of Rancho Valle de San José, which later became part of Warner Ranch. Portilla abandoned the rancho and J. J. Warner was awarded the land grant.*

tempt to oust the Indians from the hot springs, perhaps because many of them worked for him on the rancho.

Don Juan's house was still standing in 1968 on Highway S2, the road to Borrego, about a mile east of Highway 79. The structure and an old adobe and wood barn were enclosed by a chain-link fence.

A historical marker noted that Gen. Stephen W. Kearny and his troops passed there in 1846 just before the Battle of San Pasqual, and the Mormon Battalion a month later. The first Butterfield stage stopped at the rancho October 6, 1858, en route from Tipton, Missouri, to San Francisco—2,600 miles in twenty-four days.

A little more than a mile farther east and a few hundred feet north of the road was another old adobe once believed by some to have been the But-

terfield station. A marker so proclaimed it, but historians later agreed it was built after the Butterfield route had been moved in 1861. It was known as the Kimball-Wilson station and was operated as a trading post until 1908. The building was on Warner Ranch land.

Don Juan José Warner, often called Juan Largo—Long John—because of his height of six feet three inches, was not at his rancho the day General Kearny arrived with his tired and tattered troops. Warner was in jail in San Diego on a charge that he had consorted with the enemy. He was soon exonerated and returned to the rancho.

William Marshall, Don Juan's *mayordomo*, a deserter from the sailing ship *Hopewell*, provided the troops with food and supplies. Marshall, who was married to an Indian woman, was believed to have instigated the Indian raid on Pauma Rancho a few days later when eleven rancheros, fleeing after the Battle of San Pasqual, were captured and taken to the ranchería at Agua Caliente, where they were murdered.

The night of November 22, 1851, Warner's ranchhouse was attacked by Indians. Richard F. Pourade in his book, *The Silver Dons*, vividly described the battle by Warner, a hired man and an Indian servant boy against a band of 100 Indians. Don Juan had been warned of an impending attack and had sent his wife and children to San Diego.

When their ammunition ran out the three managed to reach their horses, which had been kept saddled for just such an emergency. The hired man was killed but Warner and the boy escaped.

The Indians burned the house, drove off cattle and horses, then rode to Agua Caliente, where they murdered four Americans who had gone from San Diego to the hot springs to rest. Warner later repaired the house.

When troops from San Diego reached the rancho, they found the buildings in ruins and the bodies of two Indians. They went on to Agua Caliente, where they burned the ranchería.

A few days later, Sheriff Agoston Haraszthy and a posse captured Marshall and two Indian companions, one of them Warner's servant boy, who had escaped during the Indian attack on Warner's and had rejoined his Indian friends. A court-martial convicted the men of inciting an Indian uprising and the two were hanged December 13 in San Diego. The boy was found guilty of giving false testimony and was sentenced to receive twenty-five lashes.

Don Juan and his family left the rancho in 1855, moving to Los Angeles, where he was prominent in civic and business affairs until his death in 1895. He had been a state senator and a member of the

The southeastern section of Warner Valley is shown in this aerial view, with the San Felipe road at left and highway to Borrego at right. The hot springs and resort are on the far side of the mountain at the top center.

Don Juan José Warner, grantee of Rancho San José del Valle and Rancho Valle de San José, posed for this photograph with some of his Indian vaqueros. Warner was called Juan Largo, or Long John. He died in 1895.

This was the Kimball-Wilson trading post on rancho land about a mile east of the Warner ranchhouse. A plaque once proclaimed it was a Butterfield Stage stop, but historians later agreed this probably was an error.

first county Board of Supervisors in San Diego.

Warner was in financial difficulties before leaving San Diego. Many small parcels of the rancho had been sold to satisfy liens and the last of his vast land holdings had been disposed of by 1861.

John G. Downey, a former governor, and Louis Phillips purchased the various segments of the rancho in 1875, restoring its original boundaries. Downey later became the sole owner. After Downey's death, the Pacific Light & Power Co. of Los Angeles bought the rancho.

In 1903, the Indians were moved from their ancient home at Agua Caliente to Pala, where the government purchased 3,438 acres of land for a new reservation. Agua Caliente was their ancient home, but the federal government would not, or could not, buy this land for them. So the Army took the 200 men, women and children from the ranchería and marched them to their new home.

In 1911, William G. Henshaw acquired the property and constructed a reservoir called Lake Henshaw.

The Warner Resort Co. was operating the 3,000-acre guest ranch in the 1960's. The company was owned by the Henshaw Investment Co. of San Francisco.

The remainder of the rancho was owned by the Vista Irrigation Co., except for the 697-acre Mataguay Ranch ten miles northeast of Santa Ysabel, which was purchased in 1958 for the San Diego Council of Boy Scouts.

More than half a million dollars was raised by public subscription to purchase and develop Mataguay. There was a large lodge, lakes, swimming pools and camping sites.

El Tejón Cattle Co. of Bakersfield, one of the largest cattle companies in California and with ranches also in Arizona and New Mexico, leased the Warner Ranch and grazed several thousand cattle there.

Don Juan José Warner might feel ill at ease if he could enter the ornate resort lodge on his old rancho today—but he would feel right at home on the range with a branding crew. For the Tejón cattlemen, disdaining the modern chute-branding method, roped and branded on the range as did the *vaqueros* a century ago.

5

San Dieguito Rancho

Theodoso Osuna was born in Spain and came to San Diego in the 1780's, riding a mule up the Baja California peninsula from La Paz. He married an Indian girl, Luguarda Quisques, and their first child was Juan María Osuna, born in 1785.

Only a few decades later this son became Don Juan María Osuna, the first *alcalde* of San Diego in 1834, and justice of the peace in 1839. He had been a soldier, a corporal in the San Diego Company, and took part in the brief revolt in 1831.

In 1840 and 1841 he was given provisional grants to San Dieguito Rancho, twenty-five miles north of San Diego and three miles from the ocean. This tract, 8,824 acres of excellent grazing land, he stocked with cattle and horses. His grant was made permanent in 1845 by the last Mexican governor, Pío Pico.

There is disagreement over the meaning of the name San Dieguito. Some say it means "little San Diego" and came from St. Didacus de Alcalá, after whom San Diego itself was named. Others contend it was derived from the name of St. James the Lesser.

This rancho, where once the only buildings were an adobe ranchhouse and a small adobe barn, in modern days became dotted with scores of small ranchos, country estates and beautiful homes, paved roads, a community center, a golf course and a business district. San Dieguito Rancho became Rancho Santa Fe.

The Osunas were prominent in early-day San Diego County civil and political life, and after secularization of the missions in 1834, Don Juan became *mayordomo* and administrator of the San Diego Mission. He had a daughter, Felipa, who married Don Juan María Marrón, grantee of Agua Hedionda Rancho, and two sons, Leandro and Ramón. Both sons fought with Andrés Pico at the Battle of San Pasqual in 1846. Leandro reportedly killed Capt. Benjamin Moore of the American forces in hand-to-hand combat.

Don Juan María Osuna died in March, 1851, at the age of sixty-six. He was buried in the old cemetery in Old Town.

Leandro Osuna, who inherited the rancho, killed himself with a pistol in his home at Old Town eight years later. He had incurred the enmity of many of

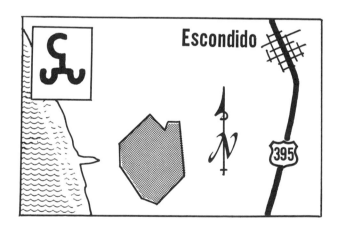

the Indians and believed one of them had slipped poison into his food. He had been ill several days when he took his life.

Leandro Osuna's son Julio then took over control of the rancho. He had married Josefa, daughter of Philip Crosthwaite, business man and former sheriff of San Diego County. Crosthwaite was the first worshipful master of San Diego Lodge No. 35, F. & A. M., which was the first Masonic Lodge chartered in Southern California.

Julio Osuna and his family lived in the Leandro Osuna house a short distance from the ranchhouse

Juliana López Osuna, widow of Juan María Osuna, filed this diseño *in claiming San Dieguito Rancho.*

built by Don Juan. Ramón Osuna, one of Julio's sons, was born in this house in 1882. In 1968 he told of working as a vaquero on the rancho and recalled that Julio used the brand O-J rather than that of his grandfather and great-grandfather.

Both of the Osuna houses were restored and remodeled. That of Don Juan was at one time owned by Bing Crosby; the other was owned by Mr. and Mrs. H. C. Morton of Los Angeles.

Members of the Osuna family lived on San Dieguito Rancho until 1906, by which time their holdings had shrunk to about 200 acres.

The Santa Fe Land Improvement Co., a subsidiary of the Santa Fe Railroad, bought up all the original acreage of the land grant and changed its name to Rancho Santa Fe. Thousands of eucalyptus trees were planted on the rolling hills, the Santa Fe hoping to use the trees as ties for railroad construction work. When the ties were put into service, however, it was discovered the wood would not hold the heavy railroad spikes.

Col. Ed Fletcher, pioneer San Diego developer, and W. G. Henshaw then entered the picture. They owned water rights and land east of the rancho. Backed by W. E. Hodges, vice president of the Santa Fe Railroad, they formed the San Dieguito Mutual Water Co. and constructed Hodges Dam. It was completed in 1917, and the water it provided assured Rancho Santa Fe the supply it needed to make it one of the state's finest suburban developments.

The Osunas had always been lovers of fine horses, and could these rancheros of a century ago return today they would be pleased to see that many of the present owners of their lands also are horsemen.

A. H. Smith owned this farm and dairy on land that was a part of San Dieguito Rancho. Members of the Osuna family lived on the rancho until 1906, when their remaining holdings totaled only about two hundred acres.

6

Jamacha Rancho

Apolinaria Lorenzana was a devout woman who spent most of her life in working for the Catholic Church and in helping the Indians. She came to San Diego about the year 1800, one of eight youngsters from an orphanage in Mexico to be placed in foster homes.

Little is known of her early life here, except that she helped the mission fathers, nursed the sick, and was a sincere friend to the Indians, who called her *La Beata*, "the devout one."

History does not record why she was given—nor why she wanted—the 8,881-acre Jamacha Rancho, the boundaries of which extended from Rancho de la Nación almost to El Cajón Rancho. Nevertheless, in 1840 Gov. Juan Bautista Alvarado granted her the land.

The rancho had been the site of an Indian ranchería. Jamacha is an Indian word meaning "wild squash vine" or "gourd." It is commonly pronounced ham'-a-shaw, although some contend the last syllable should be accented and pronounced cha.

Doña Apolinaria had few horses and cattle, compared to the thousands that many of her neighboring Dons owned. She had lived on the rancho for several years prior to receiving the grant. The mother and sisters of Don Pío Pico fled to her home just before the Indian attack on Jamul Rancho in

1837. The women then continued to San Diego in their ox-drawn *carreta*, but Doña Apolinaria refused to leave her rancho, apparently having no fear of the Indians.

In 1843, Gov. Manuel Micheltorena granted Doña Apolinaria the tiny La Cañada de los Coches Rancho, which was within the boundaries of El Cajón Rancho. There she raised pigs for the mission fathers.

In 1852, Jamacha Rancho became the property of A. R. Eddy, who had been an army lieutenant, and Frank Ames, through some process Doña Apolinaria never fully understood. Robert Kelly, who later purchased Agua Hedionda Rancho, had been her *mayordomo*.

Doña Apolinaria later deeded Los Coches to the Catholic Church, and moved to Santa Barbara, where she died, blind and destitute, at an advanced age.

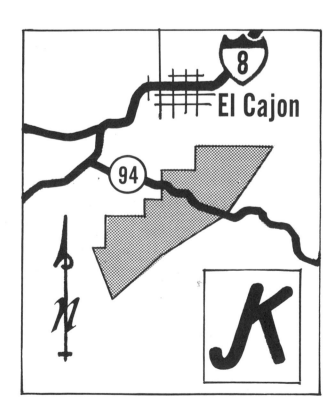

Through the years Jamacha Rancho was cut up into many parcels. The largest of these, 3,730 acres in the north central part of the rancho, was purchased in the late 1800's by Joseph W. Sefton, San Diego banker.

The tract, called Monte Vista Ranch, was sold in 1943 to Thomas E. Sharp for about $115,000.

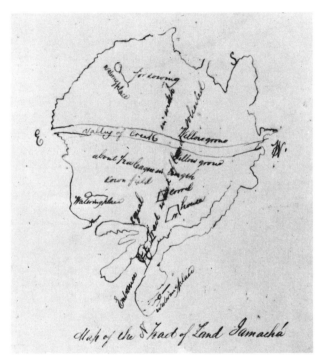

Apolinaria Lorenzana's diseño *shows the Sweetwater River flowing through the Jamacha Rancho.*

In 1965 the ranch was sold to Monte Vista Properties for about $5,000,000. Stockholders of this corporation included a number of Hollywood personalities, among them Danny Kaye, Meredith Willson and Carl Reiner.

In 1968 the ranch was being held for suburban development, with the range lands leased temporarily for cattle grazing.

No trace remained of the adobe ranchhouse where Doña Apolinaria had lived, and residents of the area had never heard of any adobe ruins which might have marked the site.

Some believed the house was just north of the Sweetwater River, on the Monte Vista Ranch. However, those who had ridden over practically every foot of the ranch never found any trace of the house.

At the junction of Jamacha Road and Willow Glen Drive the Cottonwood Country Club was constructed. Adjoining the golf course was the Ivanhoe quarter-horse ranch owned by Mr. and Mrs. David C. Campbell and their daughter, Dr. Jean Immenschuh, a veterinarian.

Farther west on the old Jamacha grant, near the intersection of Jamacha Boulevard and Sweetwater Springs Road, was the spring which became famous in the late 1880's. Known as Isham's Spring, its mineral waters were claimed as a cure-all for ills.

In 1887, Capt. Charles Fitzallen of the ship *Challenger*, out of Cardiff, Wales, arrived in San Diego. He was suffering from scurvy and sought the advice of Dr. P. C. Remondino, a leading physician. The doctor suggested he work as a sheepherder until he regained his health. George Neale, who grazed a large flock near the base of San Miguel Mountain, hired him. One of their camps was at this spring and its waters seemed to work wonders for the sea captain.

Dr. Remondino analyzed the water and said it contained certain mineral and healing properties. Alfred H. Isham, a traveling hardware salesman, heard of the spring and contracted with a San Francisco company, which then owned the rancho, to sell the water.

Isham erected a small bottling plant and began advertising "Isham's California Water of Life—the Fountain of Youth." He charged one dollar a gallon. Isham was so successful that he soon enlarged his scope of activities to several eastern states.

Then, returning from the East, Isham found that his business had been taken over by George Sanford, representing the rancho owners. In some manner Isham managed to regain control and soon again left for the East. And Sanford again took possession of the business. On Isham's return this time there was gunplay. Sanford fired a revolver, missing Isham but fatally wounding Captain Fitzallen, who had been working at the bottling plant.

Isham assumed control again; soon he was shipping spring water by the trainload. Then came the

Isham's Spring in 1968 still produced the water which made it famous in the 1800's. Alfred H. Isham bottled and sold the water for one dollar a gallon as Isham's California Water of Life—the Fountain of Youth.

The overflow from Isham's Spring formed ponds just off Jamacha Boulevard, near Sweetwater Springs Road. The water was claimed to have mineral and healing properties; its promoter made—and lost—a fortune.

panic of 1907 and the medicinal water bubble burst. Isham had been spending money as fast as he made it and had no reserve to fall back on. A winter shipment to the East had frozen and all the containers had burst. The final blow came with publication of an "expose" type article in the now defunct Collier's Magazine that said Isham's wild claims for his water were false.

Isham's business collapsed and he left San Diego, never to return. There was a time after Isham's departure when the spring was a popular picnic spot. The property which included the spring was owned in 1968 by Fred J. Hansen, land developer. The spring, then weed- and brush-choked, had kept up its steady flow for more than a century.

Farther west, Dictionary Hill and the shopping center on Sweetwater Road were within the Jamacha grant.

An enterprising dictionary salesman bought the hill about 1920 and gave away a lot with each book sold. There was an old wagon road up the north side, but residential development was delayed until the 1960's, when streets on the south side of the hill were paved and construction of homes started. The hill affords a wonderful view of South Spring Valley, La Presa, Sweetwater Lake, Point Loma and the ocean.

Dictionary Hill marked the north boundary of the grant in this area. La Presa is within the grant, as well as Sweetwater Lake, but the home development west of Sweetwater Road is not, nor the Spring Valley area north of the hill.

The 3,730-acre Monte Vista Ranch was the largest remaining tract in Jamacha Rancho. Rows of palm trees at left and center once marked the county road. Ranch lands in 1968 were being held for future development.

7

Los Vallecitos de San Marcos Rancho

Los Vallecitos de San Marcos Rancho was an elongated, irregular shaped, hill-and-valley beauty spot of 8,877 acres stretching from near the modern city of Escondido almost to Vista.

Before the secularization of the missions in 1834, the rancho was one of the cattle-grazing tracts claimed by San Luis Rey Mission. In 1840, Los Vallecitos de San Marcos, or the little valleys of St. Mark, was granted to Don José María Alvarado by Gov. Juan Bautista Alvarado.

Don José married Luguarda Osuna, daughter of Don Juan María Osuna, grantee of San Dieguito Rancho, now Rancho Santa Fe.

Don José was killed by Indians a few days after the Battle of San Pasqual in 1846. He was one of a group of eleven rancheros captured by an Indian band in the home of José Antonio Serrano, owner of Pauma Rancho. The men were taken to an Indian rancheria at Agua Caliente, on Rancho San José del Valle, and slain.

William Marshall, *mayordomo* at Rancho San José del Valle, now the Warner Ranch, had been a suitor for the beautiful Luguarda's hand, and he was blamed by many as the instigator of the raid. When Marshall was sentenced to be executed in San Diego

in 1851 as a leader in the Garra Indian revolt, he asked Doña Luguarda to walk with him to the gallows and she did so.

She later married Luis Machado, owner of Buena Vista Rancho.

History is not clear as to occupancy of San Marcos Rancho during the next few years. However, Lorenzo Soto, who fought against the Americans in 1846-47, was the next owner; he was a claimant for the rancho before the U.S. Land Commission and was given a patent in 1883.

The rancho later was purchased by Cave J. Couts, former Army officer, who was the owner of nearby Guajome Rancho and who had purchased Buena Vista Rancho. Couts trail-herded large numbers of cattle to San Francisco during the Gold Rush.

In the land boom of the 1880's the San Marcos Land Co. was formed by Jacob Gruendike, San

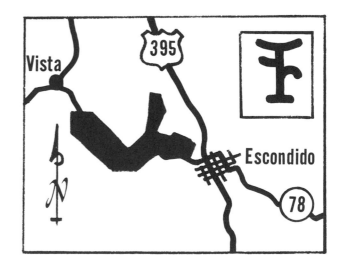

Diego banker, and several other business men. The company bought San Marcos Rancho for a reported $233,000 and laid out a townsite about two and one-half miles west of the present town, near the intersection of Grand Avenue and Rancho Santa Fe Road.

Many houses were built, as well as a hotel, post office and several stores. In 1892 there were eighty-seven registered voters. Then came disaster for the little boom town—the Santa Fe Railroad established

These buildings formed the business section of San Marcos just before the turn of the century. In 1901 the town and most of its buildings were moved to its present site, about two and a half miles to the east.

This hay-bailing crew operated on the rolling hills of Los Vallecitos de San Marcos Rancho about 1900. Hay was fed to the rancho horses and cattle when summer heat parched the thousands of acres of pasture lands.

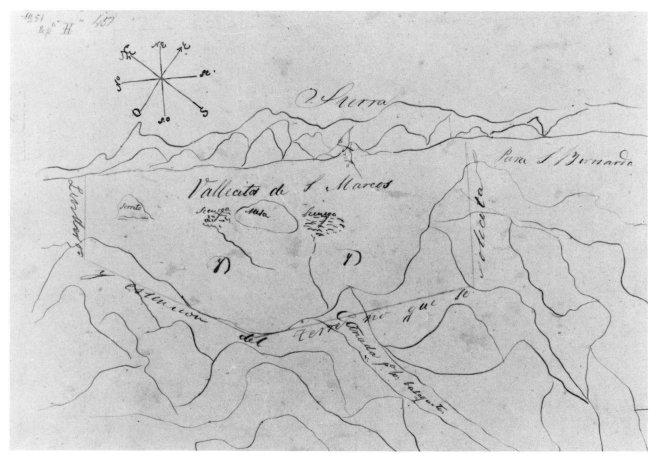

Don José María Alvarado, grantee of Los Vallecitos de San Marcos Rancho, was killed by Indians. His heirs sold the rancho to Lorenzo Soto, who presented this diseño *to the Land Commission claiming legal ownership.*

its depot where the city is now. The old town was abandoned in 1901 and many of its buildings were moved to the new location.

Amos Trussell, son and grandson of early-day San Diego County dairymen, was born on the San Pasqual Valley ranch purchased by his grandfather in 1895. In 1910 his father, Ray Trussell, bought La Ciénega Ranch, which was on the original San Marcos grant.

About 1937 a silk factory was constructed at San Marcos, with 400 acres of land devoted to the growing of mulberry trees on which to raise silk worms. The advent of rayon spelled the end for the silk project.

In 1945 a junior college was voted, to be situated in San Marcos and to be called Palomar Junior College. Classes first were held in Vista, and the present campus was placed in operation in 1950, with additional buildings added since that time.

About eighty per cent of the original land grant came within the city limits of San Marcos. Scores of dairies, citrus and chicken ranches took over the range where once long-horned cattle grazed.

But the old rancho did not become entirely an agricultural area. There were many small industries, stores and restaurants. The largest single development was Lake San Marcos, a 1,500-acre tract, most of which was on the old land grant.

8

Rancho Santa Margarita y las Flores

Don Pío Pico, twice governor of California during Mexican rule, gave many of San Diego County's land grant ranchos to friends and relatives—but he and his younger brother, Andrés, received the choicest grant of all. Rancho Santa Margarita y las Flores.

The acreage totaled 133.440 and stretched from Oceanside into Orange and Riverside counties, and eastward to Fallbrook. There were thirty-five miles of coastline, seven rivers and streams, seven small lakes and three mountain ranges.

Today the greater part of this huge grant, 125,000 acres, is the world's largest amphibious training base for the United States Marine Corps, Camp Pendleton.

Pío Pico was a politician and a gambler; Don Andrés was later to become a general in the Mexican army in California.

Both brothers were cattlemen and Rancho Santa Margarita y las Flores prospered under their ownership. At one time their livestock included 10,000 cattle, 2,000 horses and 15,000 sheep. They made many cattle drives to cities as far north as San Francisco.

The huge rancho was practically a principality,

where they ruled from a beautiful adobe home on a knoll overlooking a small lake. They numbered their *vaqueros*, field workers and servants by the score. Their barns and corrals, a short distance from the house, covered many acres. The original home, with some modernization, became the residence of the commandant of Camp Pendleton.

The Spanish explorer, Gaspar de Portolá, soon after arriving in San Diego with Father Junípero Serra in 1769, started the march northward to Monterey. On the sixth day, July 20, his party of seventy-four made camp in the valley where the Marine Corps headquarters is now situated. Father Juan Crespí, one of the party, told in his diary how the area was named Santa Margarita—it was discovered on the day of Saint Margaret.

The area later came under the jurisdiction of

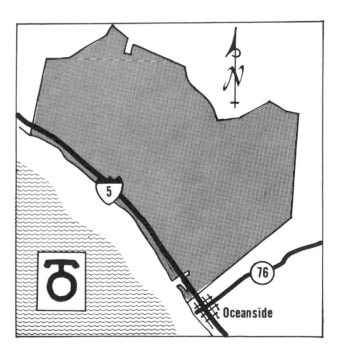

Mission San Luis Rey. The mission fathers supervised construction of an *asistencia*, or outpost of the mission, in 1822. Parts of the walls of this building, about a mile from the ocean, were still standing in 1968. About 300 Indians lived in adobe and brush huts, making a good-sized village around the *asistencia*. They called it Las Flores, or "the flowers."

Graceful arches mark the walkway to the chapel at the U.S. Marine Corps Base, Camp Pendleton. Adobe structure on Rancho Santa Margarita, built as winery by the Pico brothers; also later was blacksmith shop.

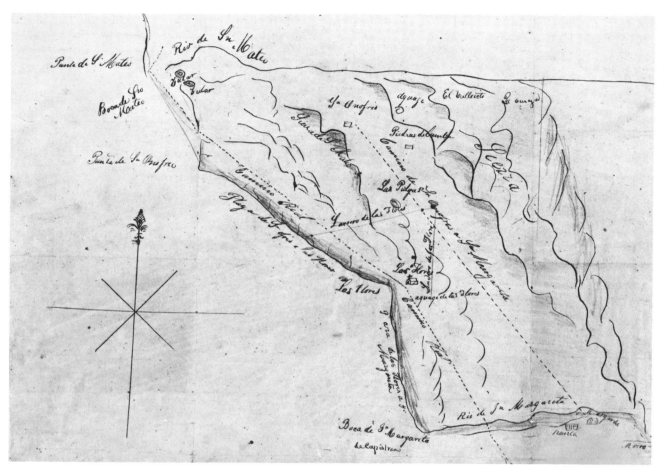

Don Pío Pico and his brother, Gen. Andrés Pico, presented this diseño *to the U.S. Land Commission in support of their claim to Rancho Santa Margarita y las Flores. This was the largest grant made in the county.*

After secularization of the missions in 1834, Las Flores became a *pueblo libre,* or free town, under Indian control, and it remained as such until after the Picos took over Rancho Santa Margarita.

In 1838, Gov. Juan Bautista Alvarado's rule was threatened by Carlos Carrillo, brother of a San Diego school teacher, who had an appointment as governor from the Mexican congress.

Carlos Carrillo took the oath of office December 6 in Los Angeles, and the action was ratified at San Diego three days later, as related by Richard F. Pourade in his book, *The Silver Dons.*

Governor Alvarado refused to relinquish his post and two months later Gen. José Castro defeated a force led by Carrillo, and José Antonio Pico and Andrés Pico, brothers of Pío Pico, in a battle at San

Buenaventura. Carrillo's forces fled but seventy men were captured, including Andrés Pico.

A short time later Castro again met Carrillo in a brief battle at Las Flores, where the Carrillo forces from San Diego, with three cannons, were entrenched at the *asistencia.* Only one shot was fired, then the two leaders talked for three days under a flag of truce. Carrillo finally agreed to disband his troops.

Pío Pico was born in 1801 at San Gabriel Mission, where his father, José María Pico, was a non-commissioned officer in the guard detachment. The family later moved to San Diego, where Andrés was born in 1810.

The Pico brothers were appointed administrators of San Luis Rey Mission, and in 1841, restored to

27

the good graces of the governor, they received from him the grant to Rancho Santa Margarita. This grant was for 89,642 acres; however, in 1844 Las Flores section was added, making a total of 133,440 acres.

In 1845-46 Pío Pico was again governor. He had held that post for twenty days in 1832. As the American forces began to take control of the state in 1846 he fled to Mexico. His brother, Andrés, by then a general in the Mexican army, commanded the force of Californios which attacked Gen. Stephen Kearny's troops at the Battle of San Pasqual. Later, after surrendering to Gen. John C. Frémont, he signed the Capitulation of Cahuenga Treaty, closing the Mexican War in California.

With both Picos away from the rancho, their brother-in-law, Don Juan Forster, was in nominal charge. Don Juan was an English trader who had married Doña Ysidora Pico. Their home was on a large rancho near San Juan Capistrano.

Don Juan had lent Pío Pico, who had returned from Mexico in 1848, large sums to pay his gam-

bling debts, and in 1864 he offered to pay $14,000 and assume other debts totaling more than $40,000 if Don Pío would sign over Rancho Santa Margarita y las Flores to him. Andrés Pico had sold his share to Pío two years before. Pío agreed. Pío Pico, almost penniless, died in Los Angeles at the age of ninety-three.

Forster immediately assumed control of the rancho and spent large sums on improvements. He had three sons—Francisco (Chico), Marcus and John. Don Juan gave Marcus the land around the old Las Flores *asistencia* as a wedding present. A few hundred yards east of the Indian village, Marcus, in 1865, built a sixteen-room Monterey-style two-story home of adobe and wood. Adobe bricks and timbers from the *asistencia* were used in much of the construction.

All of the Forsters were famed for their hospitality. Both Las Flores ranchhouse and the Santa Margarita ranchhouse were the scenes of countless fiestas and other social gatherings. Marcus Forster's old home, still in good condition in 1968, was only a

Sketch made in 1913 of the rear wing of the big adobe house built by the Pico brothers on Rancho Santa Margarita y las Flores. Servants' quarters and bunkhouse for the vaqueros *were in separate buildings near by.*

Gen. Andrés Pico, soldier and ranchero, led Californios against U.S. troops at Battle of San Pasqual.

hundred feet from old Highway 101; the Santa Margarita ranchhouse is about seven miles farther east and about nine miles from Highway 5.

Don Juan Forster mortgaged the rancho in 1881 to Charles Crocker of San Francisco for $207,000. Six months later Forster died. His sons sold the property the following year to Richard O'Neill for $450,000. The latter immediately deeded the property to James L. Flood, who had provided the purchase money. O'Neill supervised the rancho and in 1906 was deeded an undivided half interest as a reward for his many years of service.

The Henry Magee family lived in Las Flores Ranchhouse for many years. Henry Magee had come to California in 1847 as a lieutenant in the Union Army. Two years later he married Victoria de Pedrorena, a daughter of Miguel de Pedrorena.

Doña Victoria became one of the heirs to El Cajón Rancho when her father died in 1850.

The Magees purchased the Castro Ranch, overlooking San Luis Rey Valley, and later moved to Las Flores, where the former army officer, under a lease arrangement with O'Neill, developed several thousand acres for raising of grain and lima beans. The Magees had nine children.

After the death of Henry Magee in 1887, the eldest daughter, Jane, and her brothers and sisters supervised the ranch. Doña Victoria had died before that time.

President Franklin D. Roosevelt visited Las Flores in 1942 after the land had been taken over by the Marine Corps. He granted life-time occupancy of the ranchhouse and 1.6-acre site to the Magees of that generation. Mrs. Ruth Magee, the widow of Louis Magee, was the last to survive; she died in March, 1968.

Ruins of Las Flores *asistencia* were designated as a California Historical Landmark and efforts were made to have the state take over the old ranchhouse and grounds as a state park.

O'Neill died in 1910 at the age of eighty-five. His son Jerome purchased the interests of his mother, two sisters and brother. Jerome had been crippled in childhood by infantile paralysis and walked with great difficulty. Once on a horse, however, he was the equal of most *vaqueros*. He mounted with the aid of a special platform he had built near the front entrance to the ranchhouse.

The 1916 flood caused the Santa Margarita River to overflow and the little lake near the ranchhouse spread out to inundate the barns and corrals. The ranchhouse was on a knoll but it was surrounded by water.

In 1931 it was reported that the crime syndicate headed by Al Capone had made an offer to purchase Santa Margarita. The syndicate presumably was attracted by the thirty-five miles of coastline. Although the offer was refused, bootleggers during the prohibition years made extensive use of the lonely beaches in landing their liquor cargoes, which they cached in the nearby hills for distribution later by truck.

Combat Marines charge uphill in training exercise at Camp Pendleton, which once was Rancho Santa Margarita y las Flores. Among the trees is remodeled Pico adobe, in 1968 the home of camp commandant.

In May of 1941 the United States government bought 9,000 acres of the rancho to establish the Naval Ammunition Depot at Fallbrook. A year later the remaining acreage in San Diego County was purchased by the government for $4,239,062.

Camp Pendleton was dedicated September 25, 1942, with President Roosevelt officiating. The camp was named for Gen. Joseph H. Pendleton, USMC, who in retirement, made his home in Coronado.

As the President inspected the old Pico ranchhouse he was greatly impressed by the charm of its early California architecture and furnishings. Pausing in one of the bedrooms he remarked, "Reserve this room for the next ex-President of the United States." Although he never slept in the room, it has always been called the President's Room.

Mr. Roosevelt also expressed the hope that this beautiful home would be fully restored and kept in perfect condition by each succeeding commandant of the base. This hope has been fulfilled, as could be seen on a visit to the former rancho in the 1960's.

The ranchhouse of twenty rooms was built around a flower-filled patio where many of the trees and shrubs were planted more than a hundred years ago.

All the roofs were red-tiled and many of the floors

were of polished tile. All of the rooms were beautifully furnished in a style combining modernity with the historic past of the big home. In the Cowboy Room several old Mexican saddles hung on the walls, as well as bridles, old rifles, and branding irons.

A 115-year-old bell, once used at Las Flores *asistencia*, hung from the arch over the front entrance to the ranchhouse. A short distance from the house was the chapel, a long, arched adobe structure rebuilt by the Marines. During the Pico regime the building was a winery; Richard O'Neill converted it into a blacksmith shop.

Across the driveway at the rear of the ranchhouse was a long, narrow building divided into small rooms; this was where the *vaqueros* once lived. Two of the rooms were remodeled as a small museum, where old branding irons, bridles, photographs and Indian relics were displayed. The barns and corrals once were just beyond this building, but they were replaced by a tennis court, shade trees and lawns.

What once was Rancho Santa Margarita y las Flores became the world's largest Marine amphibious training base, but the romantic flavor of the Days of the Dons was not entirely lost.

One might wish that Don Pío Pico and his brother, Gen. Andrés Pico, could have seen their huge rancho in the 1960's. They would have been pleased to see the care given their old home—but above all, they would have been impressed by the military might represented on the base.

And perhaps General Pico might have wished he had commanded a few battalions of Californios like the modern-day Marines in those days more than a century ago when he was trying to keep the American forces from occupying California.

9

San Bernardo Rancho

San Bernardo Rancho, only a few miles north of San Diego, once was a 17,763-acre cattle ranch, comprising two Mexican land grants given to Joseph F. Snook, a British sea captain, in 1842 and 1845.

More than a century later it was still San Bernardo Rancho, but included in the original boundaries were many small farms and a 2,000-acre housing development, Rancho Bernardo.

The cattle that roamed the hills and valleys of San Bernardo Rancho in 1968 were fewer, and they had less than 4,000 acres on which to graze. And the later Black Angus cattle had little resemblance to the rangy longhorns whose hides were more valuable than their meat.

The rancho's first owner, Captain Snook, had spent many years along the California coast as master of various ships before becoming a Mexican citizen in 1833 and changing his name to José Francisco Snook.

In 1842 he was granted two square leagues of land by Gov. Juan Bautista Alvarado. His land adjoined Rancho Rincón del Diablo, now Escondido, the site of which was owned by Don Juan Bautista Alvarado, whose name was the same as the governor's and they were distantly related. Snook gave up the sea to become a ranchero and married Don

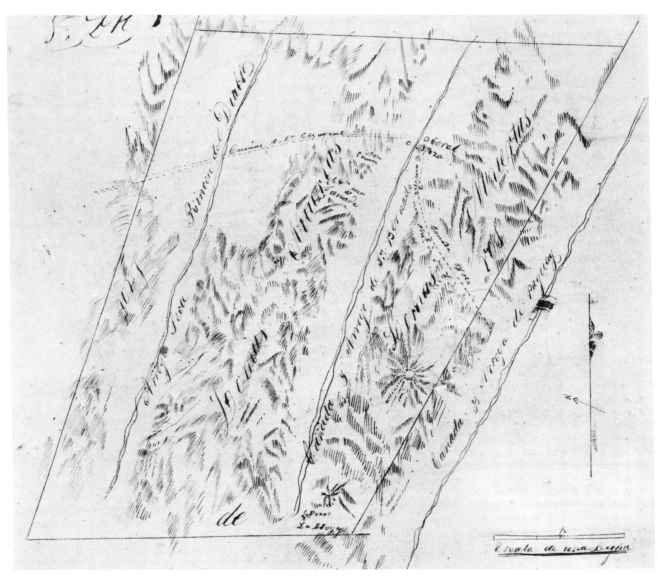

María Antonia Snook, widow of Capt. Joseph F. Snook, filed this diseño *as claimant for San Bernardo Rancho. Doña María was the daughter of the owner of Rancho Rincón del Diablo. It adjoined San Bernardo Rancho.*

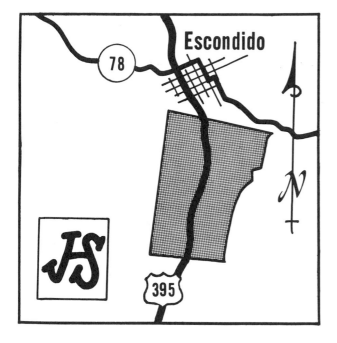

Juan's daughter, María Antonia. In 1845 he was given the second grant by Gov. Pío Pico.

After the Battle of San Pasqual, which took place only a few miles from the Snook ranchhouse, General Kearny's tattered forces began their march toward the coast and San Diego. That night they reached San Bernardo Rancho and found the ranchhouse deserted except for a few Indians. There they killed chickens to feed the wounded and rounded up a few cattle.

After a short rest the troopers moved on down the valley, but a small force of Californios suddenly appeared riding out of a ravine ahead. There was considerable gunfire and the cattle were stampeded, then the Americans, carrying their wounded, dragged themselves up a rocky hill where they set up rock barricades for protection. They dug holes in the river bed for water and killed the fattest of their remaining mules for food.

This rocky point became known as Mule Hill and was plainly visible from Highway 395.

The Americans' situation was desperate. Kit Carson, Lieut. Edward F. Beale and an Indian volunteered to carry a plea for help to Commodore R. F. Stockton in San Diego. They got through the enemy lines and the commodore dispatched 180 men.

Meanwhile at Mule Hill, the Californios attempted to drive a herd of wild horses through the camp. but the animals were turned aside. The Americans were on the hill three days before the rescue party appeared. Two days later they were safe in San Diego.

Captain Snook died a few years later and his widow married Henry Clayton, who came to San Diego with the Mexican Boundary Survey in 1849 and was San Diego County's first surveyor. The Claytons died without leaving any children and the huge rancho was split up into many parcels.

The little town of Bernardo sprang up in the valley above Hodges Dam, near Highway 395. There was a store, a blacksmith shop, post office, and a one-room school. Bernardo was inundated after Lake Hodges was built in 1917; water backed up the valley for several miles. The San Dieguito Mutual Water Co., organized by Ed Fletcher and financed

The little town of Bernardo was built close to the river just east of Highway 395. There was a store, black-smith shop and several homes. Construction in 1917 of Hodges Dam resulted in the inundation of the town.

This adobe house near Highway 395 may have been the home of the Snooks family on San Bernardo Rancho. Another adobe, also on the rancho, was torn down; it was built on the site of Escondido's Kit Carson Park.

Aerial view of part of the Rancho Bernardo housing development constructed on part of San Bernardo Rancho. The original acreage of the rancho was 17,763 and consisted of two land grants, made in 1842 and 1845.

by the Santa Fe Railroad, bought 3,000 acres of rancho land and built the dam.

There were several adobe houses on San Bernardo Rancho, but only one remained in 1968 and it was on land owned by the city of San Diego. Another large adobe was a mile or so to the northeast, but the city destroyed the crumbling ruins, leaving only the huge stone fireplace.

The city of Escondido purchased this latter site, planning to develop a 235-acre park named in honor of Kit Carson.

S. M. Villalobos, park foreman, recalled the old adobe and believed it was the original Snooks ranchhouse, later known as the Prentice ranchhouse.

There were rocky hills about a mile and a half west of the highway where many Indian pictographs were found on huge boulders. The drawings were reddish in color and many were badly weathered; all were in the form of designs rather than pictures of humans or animals.

On the flat just below were many large stones that had been hollowed out, where Indian women ground corn or acorns a hundred years ago.

Lawrence and Donald Daley owned the rancho for many years.

The Daleys sold 2,000 acres of the original grant to Rancho Bernardo in 1961 and development of a residential community was begun. In 1968 there were 2,000 home units and a population of about 4,200.

In Rancho Bernardo Industrial Park, a multimillion-dollar plant was constructed for the National Cash Register Co. The plant site totaled 114 acres.

Black Angus cattle grazed on the few thousand acres remaining of San Bernardo Rancho in 1968. The long-horned animals of a century ago were valuable mostly for their hides and often sold for only a few dollars.

36

10

Agua Hedionda Rancho

Don Juan María Marrón ruled the Agua Hedionda Rancho in the 1840's. His 13,311 acres extended from the Pacific Ocean inland almost to Vista and from Carlsbad south to Encina Canyon.

Don Juan had been a ship's captain before coming to San Diego in the early 1820's. He soon became prominent politically and married Doña Felipa, daughter of Juan María Osuna, the first *alcalde* of the pueblo of San Diego and the owner of San Dieguito Rancho. Agua Hedionda Rancho was granted to Marrón in 1842.

During the Mexican War, Don Juan supported the Americans against many of his Mexican friends. This support caused him considerable hardship and embarrassment at times. Richard F. Pourade in his book, *The Silver Dons*, relates an incident which took place in 1846:

"One morning, along the road from the mission, came *Alcalde* Juan María Marrón, husband of Felipa Osuna, carrying a white flag. He wanted to visit his wife. Capt. Miguel de Pedrorena took him into custody, but Commodore Robert F. Stockton finally gave Felipa and her husband a pass through the lines, to go to their rancho. With their children they walked all the way to San Luis Rey Mission, where another band of Californios seized them and threatened to shoot Marrón for having collaborated with the Americans. They released him but stripped his Agua Hedionda Rancho of horses and cattle."

Several adobe homes were built on the rancho by members of the Marrón family through the years. Most of the structures have disappeared, but several were incorporated into modern residences.

One of these was the home of Carroll R. Kelly, whose grandfather was Matthew Kelly Sr., brother of the fourth owner of the rancho. Carroll Kelly farmed and raised cattle on the rancho for thirty-five years. In 1958 he rebuilt the house where Don Juan lived, reinforcing the twenty-six-inch walls and constructing additional wings along the foundation lines laid out by the original owner.

Another ancient adobe built by Juan María Marrón, grandson of the original grantee, was in ruins in 1968 but several of its walls were still standing. It was on the north side of Highway 78 less than a mile east of El Camino Real intersection, in a grove of pepper and eucalytus trees.

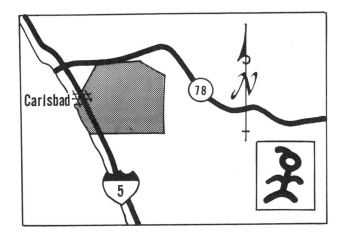

This property was owned by the Steiger family of Oceanside. John A. Steiger, a realtor, said his grandfather started making the bricks for the house about 1895. His mother, Mrs. Laura Steiger, lived in the adobe as a child. Steiger's grandmother was Doña Lorenza Serrano de Marrón, a direct descendant of José Antonio Serrano, grantee of Pauma Rancho.

On the south side of the highway, nearby, was the adobe home of Silvestre Marrón, brother of Don

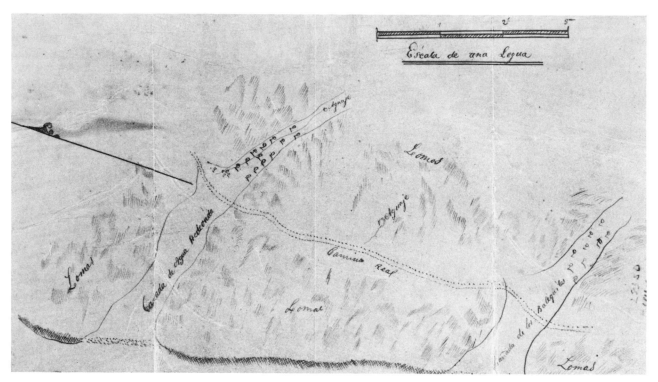

Don Juan María Marrón received the grant to the Agua Hedionda Rancho in 1842. This diseño *supported his claim to the land. Don Juan died in 1853. His widow and their four children inherited the large rancho.*

Juan. Two walls were all that remained of it in 1968.

Don Juan María Marrón died in 1853 at the age of forty-five; his widow and four children inherited Agua Hedionda Rancho, with the exception of 360 acres bequeathed to Silvestre. The latter also was given grazing rights on all of the huge rancho.

The Marróns leased Agua Hedionda Rancho to Francis Hinton in 1860 for a loan of $6,000, with José Marrón and José María Estudillo retaining the right to come and gather salt from the lagoons for their families.

In 1865, Hinton assumed ownership of the rancho. Six thousand dollars seems a small price for land worth millions today, but it was considered fair at that time, as drought had laid waste to thousands of acres of grazing land and there was no market for the starving cattle.

Hinton was born in New York in 1818. His real name was Abraham Ten Eyck de Witt Hornbeck. When he was twenty-seven years old he changed

his name, joined the Army and served throughout the Mexican War. He was a supply sergeant of Company A, 1st U.S. Dragoons. Cave Couts, later to become owner of Guajome Rancho, was a lieutenant in the same unit. Both Hinton and Couts came to California with the Boundary Commission guard.

Hinton died at the rancho in 1870. He had never been married and willed Agua Hedionda to his *mayordomo*, Robert Kelly, who also was a bachelor.

Kelly had been *mayordomo* of Jamacha Rancho on the Sweetwater River and also a merchant in San Diego. He died in 1890, leaving Agua Hedionda Rancho to his nine nephews and nieces, children of his brother, Matthew.

The last of these heirs, William Sherman Kelly, died on May 10, 1950, at the age of eighty-five. Holdings of his son, Allan, 820 acres of the Marrón grant, included the upper part of Agua Hedionda Lagoon.

From Allan Kelly's home can be seen the lagoon into which empties the creek of the same name, the

Aerial view of Encina power plant, far right, and part of the Agua Hedionda lagoon, which stretches several miles inland. This area was all part of the 13,311-acre land grant once owned by Don Juan María Marrón.

Encina power plant and the ocean. In the distance to the south is Palomar Airport which had been carved out of the original land grant. Within the same boundaries are two high hills, or mountains, which on county maps bear the historic names of Mount Kelly and Mount Hinton.

Another descendant of Matthew Kelly who owned about 400 acres of the land grant in 1968 was Mrs. Ida Dawson, wife of Clarence H. Dawson.

Mrs. Dawson's mother was Mary Emma Kelly Squires, who was a daughter of Matthew Kelly.

Although Matthew Kelly Sr. never owned Agua Hedionda Rancho, he lived on adjacent patented land, Los Quiotes Rancho, until his death. The Kelly heirs in 1922 sold Los Quiotes to a San Francisco syndicate, from which Leo Carrillo, movie actor, purchased the ranch in 1938. Carrillo died in 1961, leaving the property, 840 acres, to his adopted

daughter, Mrs. Marie Antoinette Carrillo Delpy. The actor had remodeled the old two-story Kelly adobe ranchhouse and made it into a modern showplace.

Pedro C. Carrillo, the actor's ancestor, was the grantee of Península de San Diego Rancho, now Coronado and North Island.

In December, 1968, the ranch was sold to a group of San Diego business men for $3,400,000. The partnership was to be known as Rancho Carrillo. No announcement was made at that time concerning plans of the new owners.

Agua Hedionda means "stinking water" in English. The name is supposed to have been given the area by the first Spanish explorers. The odor they reported might have come from a nearby Indian village, a sulphur spring, or possibly from decayed matter on the shores of the lagoon.

This was the old adobe ranchhouse of Don Juan María Marrón in 1920. More than forty years later the historic structure was completely renovated and modernized, original walls reinforced and new wings added.

11

Las Encinitas Rancho

The crumbling walls of the big adobe atop a slight rise in the fenced pasture were in plain sight of motorists traveling along the Encinitas-San Marcos road.

A few Hereford cattle grazed in the little valley to the east or stood drinking from the small stream that wandered down from the arroyo far up in the hills.

Did the passing motorist dismiss the sight of the time-ravaged adobe as "just another of those old broken-down farmhouses" and drive on? Or did his mind's eye visualize a rambling adobe ranchhouse of more than a century ago, where the Don of the rancho entertained at *fandangoes* and *fiestas*, and hard-riding *vaqueros* herded longhorn cattle through the hills and valleys?

The rancho once was Las Encinitas, or the "little live oaks." It was a 4,431-acre tract given by Gov. Juan Bautista Alvarado to Don Andrés Ybarra in 1842. It adjoined San Dieguito Rancho to the south and was a few miles east of the present city of Encinitas.

The crumbling adobe once was the home of the Ybarra family. The little creek just below the house furnished water for the rancho, and there was a wide, high cactus wall of the type that many rancheros in the 1800's planted around their rancho buildings to keep cattle out and to discourage Indian

attacks. Cactus also was used for corral walls when poles or logs were not available.

Ybarra had been something of a firebrand in California politics. In the brief turmoil of 1832 over the governorship he was chief of the forces of Capt. Agustín Zamorano around Los Angeles, Pío Pico had been chosen temporary governor and José María Echeandía military commander. Rule of the state was divided, with Echeandía in control in the north and Zamorano in the south. The latter sought control of the entire state and sent Ybarra north with a force of 100 men. Near San Gabriel, Ybarra came face to face with nearly 1,000 armed supporters of Echeandía. Ybarra beat a strategic retreat.

In San Diego some time later Ybarra operated a liquor store and in 1836 was named judge of the plains. This official decided disputes over cattle ownership at all roundups. A few years later

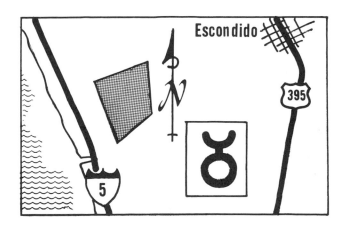

Ybarra's store was threatened with confiscation because he had not paid his taxes. After receiving Las Encinitas grant he stocked the rancho with cattle and horses and built a large adobe house.

After Ybarra sold the rancho in 1860 to two San Diego merchants, Joseph S. Mannasse and Marcus Schiller, the ranchhouse became a stage station, where travelers from San Diego stopped briefly for a meal while the stage horses were being changed for the next stretch over the hills to Mission San Luis Rey. A single wall of the old stables just east

This large adobe was once the home of Andrés Ybarra, owner of Las Encinitas Rancho. There was a wide, high cactus wall circling the building as protection from Indian attack. In 1968 the house was in ruins.

Adam Wiegand, one of the founders of the colony on Olivenhain on Las Encinitas Rancho, posed with his family for this picture in 1895. Alwin Wiegand, the boy at the right, was still a rancher in the area in 1968.

of the house was still standing after more than a hundred years.

Alwin Wiegand, eighty years old in 1968, had lived all his life on Las Encinitas Rancho or on patented land adjoining it. His brother, Herman, seventy-seven, at one time owned 1,200 acres of the original rancho.

The land occupied by the old house-stage station became part of the 2,000-acre cattle ranch operated by Alwin Wiegand's son, Dan, for Edward Rutherford of El Centro. This was the largest single tract remaining of the original land grant.

The Wiegand brothers' father, Adam, was one of the founders of a colony called Olivenhain, or olive grove, in 1885. Louis Denk was another founder.

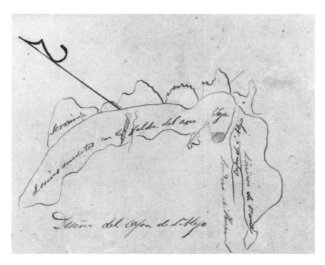

Andrés Ybarra, grantee of Las Encinitas Rancho, presented this crude map in support of his claim.

A group of Chicago and Denver families of German origin came here after seeing newspaper advertisements praising the area as a farm paradise. Bruno Denk, Louis' son, was born in Olivenhain and he recalled his parents' stories of the hard times that followed their arrival.

Denk said the original colonists bought all of Las Encinitas Rancho and laid out the Olivenhain townsite. Some historians said the colonists bought only 446 acres of the rancho from Frank and Warren Kimball, who had purchased the rancho five years before from James Currier. The latter had taken over the rancho from Mannasse and Schiller.

The colonists left the railroad at Encinitas and walked several miles across the hills to the old stage station adobe, which was their first home.

Many were so disappointed with their first view of the area that they turned back to the railroad and returned to their former homes, Denk said. The others went on to Olivenhain.

There they organized their colony, dividing a large area into five- and ten-acre tracts. A hotel, store, post office and community hall were built. The hall and hotel were still standing as late as 1968.

Trustees were selected to handle the colony's affairs and thousands of olive and citrus trees were planted. But many of the settlers, tired of the hard farm life, left, selling their lands to those who remained. Many of the latter also added to their holdings by homesteading or purchasing nearby lands already patented.

12

El Rincón del Diablo Rancho

El Rincón del Diablo seems an odd name for a large and beautiful rancho in a fertile valley only 35 miles north of San Diego. The Spanish name is translated as "the devil's corner," or "nook of the devil."

History fails to record who was responsible for naming the 12,653-acre rancho—perhaps it was the first owner, Don Juan Bautista Alvarado, who received the Mexican land grant from Gov. Manuel Micheltorena in 1843.

Whatever its origin, the name was not changed, although the rancho, as such, was swallowed up long ago by the city of Escondido.

The hill where Don Juan built his large adobe home overlooks this thriving city but the original buildings have long since gone back to the earth. Even the exact site is not known.

Don Juan was prominent in both Los Angeles and San Diego politics. In 1830 when he was forty years old, he was a *regidor*, or councilman, in Los Angeles. In 1835-36 he held the same office in San Diego, and became a member of the *diputación*, or state assembly, three years later. His daughter, María Antonia, married Capt. Joseph F. Snook, grantee of nearby San Bernardo Rancho.

Don Juan and his wife both died about 1850, and their children sold the rancho in 1857 to Judge Oliver S. Witherby. The latter came to San Diego in 1849 with the Mexican Boundary Commission. In 1850 he was named to California's first state Legislature. He later was appointed judge of the Southern District. In 1853 he was named collector of customs for the port of San Diego.

The judge operated the rancho, making his home there until 1868, when he sold the entire grant to Edward McGeary and the three Wolfskill brothers, Matthew, John and Josiah, for $8,000. The judge died at his home in San Diego in 1896.

Before the Julian-Cuyamaca gold rush of 1870, small amounts of the precious metal were found near Escondido. The Rincón del Diablo & Escondido Mining Co. was formed and a stamp mill was built. After the larger strike in the mountains the stamp mill was moved to Julian.

In 1883 the rancho was purchased by a Los Angeles syndicate for a reported $128,000. The Escondido Land & Town Co. took over the grant in 1886 and began subdividing the land into small farms. Scores of citrus groves and vineyards were planted.

In 1968 the modern city of Escondido looked like this from the air. The Orange Glen High School is at right of center. Numerous citrus groves still dotted the hills surrounding the city, which was incorporated in 1888.

This was the year the Escondido boom started. The Land & Town Co. laid out the townsite and was instrumental in getting the town incorporated in 1888, by which time Escondido was a good-sized village.

The land company built the 100-room Escondido Hotel on East Grand Avenue at a cost of $30,000. The structure was torn down in 1925 and the Palomar Memorial Hospital was constructed on the site.

The company also donated 1,000 lots for a seminary as a branch of the University of Southern California. One structure was erected at a cost of $40,000, then the property was deeded to the Escondido School District in 1894 for use as a combined elementary and high school. That original building was destroyed by fire in 1927.

Three brothers from Muscotah, Kansas, R. A., J. R. and C. E. Thomas, headed the Land & Town Co. R. A. Thomas came to San Diego in 1882; he was so impressed with the area he persuaded his brothers to sell their lumber company and bank interests in the Midwest and come to San Diego.

The Land & Town Co. drilled several wells on the rancho in 1886 to provide water for the new little city and the small farms, citrus groves and vineyards in the valley. The following year the Escondido Irrigation District was formed to build a dam and reservoir in the mountains to the northeast. This reservoir became Lake Wohlford, named for a pioneer Escondido family.

Then came the collapse of the land boom. Financial difficulties beset the irrigation company, but public-spirited Escondido Valley residents banded together to purchase, at fifty cents on the dollar, the half-million-dollar bond issue that had been sold to finance the system.

September 9, 1905, the anniversary of California Admission Day, a crowd of several thousand gathered for the bond-burning ceremony. The date was observed for many years as Grape Day, a celebration sponsored by both city residents and ranchers, with a parade, band concert, speeches, and the giving away of tons of grapes and melons to thousands of visitors.

The irrigation system was reorganized as the Escondido Mutual Water Co.

The city of Escondido was a quiet little village when this photograph was taken in 1897. The Escondido Land & Town Company took over the grant to El Rincón del Diablo Rancho in 1886 and began subdividing the land.

13

Santa María Rancho

It seems incongruous for an English merchant ship captain to become one of the Dons of early-day San Diego County, but Capt. Edward Stokes did just that.

Most of the feudal lords of the ranchos were of Mexican or Spanish descent, but there were exceptions and Captain Stokes was one of them.

That he had married Doña Refugio Ortega, daughter of Don José Joaquín Ortega, and that his father-in-law joined in his application for two large grants, undoubtedly were factors in his favor. Don José was the grandson of José Francisco Ortega, who came to San Diego from Mexico with the Portolá-Serra Expedition in 1769, and was prominent in San Diego politics. Don José Joaquín had been administrator of San Diego Mission.

So Capt. Edward Stokes became Don Eduardo Stokes and, with his father-in-law, took over the ownership of two huge ranchos, the Santa María in 1843, and the Santa Ysabel the following year.

Much of the 17,708-acre Santa María Rancho now is the city of Ramona.

Don Eduardo, while he soon acquired many of the customs of his new countrymen and learned to manage the affairs of his more than 35,000 acres, could never quite accept ranchero dress. He often wore a black velvet English hunting coat, with

black velvet trousers cut off at the knees. His Mexican and Spanish friends never questioned his choice of clothing.

Don Eduardo died in the early 1850's. His three sons—Adolfo, Eduardo and Alfredo—inherited the rancho. His widow, Doña Refugio, later married Agustín Olvera, grantee of Cuyamaca Rancho, who was a widower. One of the latter's daughters, Dolores, married Adolfo Stokes. The Stokes family built three adobe homes on Santa María Rancho, one of which was still standing in 1968 on Highway 78 near Magnolia Street, Ramona. It was owned by a Stokes descendant.

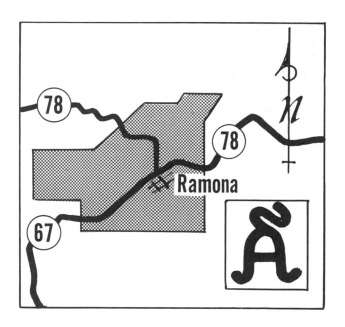

With the Julian gold rush of the 1870's, the little town of Nuevo sprang up on the Santa María; the name later was changed to Ramona. The big mule-drawn freight wagons hauling ore from the mines to a gold reduction works in National City stopped in Nuevo to change teams, and also on the return trip when they carried supplies to the gold diggings.

Bernard Echeverry, who was born in France in 1836, came to San Diego County in 1872 and became acquainted with the Stokes family. A large tract at the western end of the Santa María was

This was the family of Adolfo Stokes, one of three sons of Capt. Edward Stokes, owner with his father-in-law, José Joaquín Ortega, of Santa María Rancho. Most of the large rancho later became the town of Ramona.

Mule-drawn wagons hauling gold ore from the Julian mines to a reduction works in National City, stopped in Nuevo to change teams. On the return trip the big wagons carried back supplies to ranchos along the route.

This was the last remaining Stokes house on the Santa María Rancho in 1968. The adobe-wood home was on Highway 78 near Magnolia Street. Near the structure was an old well that flowed more than a century.

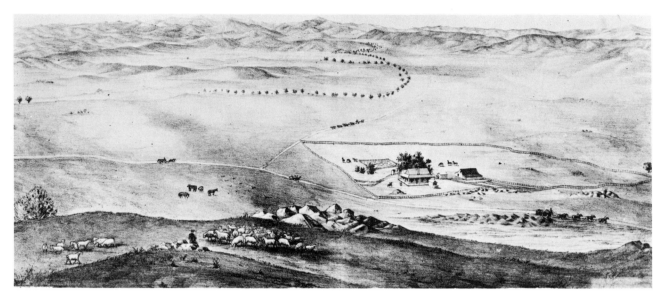

Sketch shows Bernard Echeverry's adobe house and the surrounding area. Echeverry, a sheepman from France, was given a large section of Santa María Rancho on condition he care for the Stokes and Ortega flocks.

given to him for a sheep ranch on condition he also take charge of the Stokes flocks.

Echeverry built a large adobe house. Although he had several hundred sheep, he lost almost all of his animals and other property in the drought of 1877. The adobe house was torn down in 1934.

In 1884, Milton Santee bought 6,000 acres of the rancho, and sold it in small parcels. Two years later the Santa María Land & Water Co. acquired the Ramona townsite.

Adolfo Stokes had one son and six daughters. The son was Arístides Eduardo, five of whose children lived in the area in 1968—Benjamin F. Stokes of Ramona, Edward of Oceanside, Harold and Charles of San Luis Rey, and Mrs. J. M. Higley, also of San Luis Rey.

The daughters were Connie, Mary Camille, Flora, Esperanza, Dolores and Hester. Several of their children lived in San Diego: Mrs. Catherine Grenfell and Mrs. Lucille Barber, daughters of Esperanza, and Joseph, Eugene and William Green, sons of Dolores.

Other grandchildren of Adolfo Stokes included Mrs. Dora Loveless and Mrs. Josephine Wheeler, daughters of Connie, and Mrs. Virginia Stefek, Mrs.

Ester Rocha, Mrs. Camille Valentine and Mrs. Lucille Anguisela, daughters of Mary.

Adolfo Stokes and his wife, Doña Dolores, were both buried in the old Calvary Cemetery, near Washington Street in San Diego.

There was no Captain Stokes home on Santa María Rancho, as the family lived on the Santa Ysabel, operating the two grants as one rancho. Both cattle and sheep ranged the hills and valleys.

Don Eduardo and his father-in-law believed the two ranchos joined, but a survey proved there was a strip of several thousand acres between them. About 2,000 acres of this land was owned by the Pepper family of Ballena, where B. A. Pepper later operated a gun club. He and his brother, Melvin, and two uncles, James and Sam Warnock Jr., owned the property.

Sam Warnock Sr., carried the mail on horseback between San Diego and Ft. Yuma in 1850-51, and later freighted supplies to the Julian mines. He homesteaded in the Ballena area in 1853 and bought up adjoining lands.

During the gold rush of the 1870's a townsite was laid out at Ballena and a post office was opened. The area retained its name but the post office was closed.

The Dons of the ranchos often lived in luxury in the towns. Home of Juan Bandini, southeast of the Plaza, was the finest in Old Town in the 1820's. Later, second story was added and it was used as a stage-stop hotel.

Don José Antonio Estudillo, grantee of Janal Rancho, built this large adobe home fronting on the Plaza in Old Town, San Diego, about 1827. It was remodeled, and in later days was called Ramona's Marriage Place.

Silvestre Marrón built this adobe house on Agua Hedionda Rancho, owned by his brother, Don Juan María Marrón. Remnants of the adobe walls remained in 1968 on the south side of Highway 78 near Oceanside.

Las Flores ranchhouse, constructed of adobe and wood, was built by Marcus Forster in 1865. He was a nephew of Pío and Andrés Pico. The ranchhouse, still in good repair in 1968, was near old Highway 101.

It is said that Leandro Osuna, son of Don Juan María Osuna, built this adobe on San Dieguito Rancho, which later became Rancho Santa Fe. Modernized, the house was used in 1968 by the manager of a horse ranch.

This huge oven was a part of the kitchen complex in a wing extending from the north side of the patio of Guajome Rancho. Cave J. Couts began construction of the twenty-room adobe ranchhouse about 1851.

This little adobe chapel was built about 1830 for the Agua Caliente Indians on what was later to become Rancho San José del Valle, Warner Ranch. In 1968 services were still being held there every Sunday morning.

Indians built this adobe house about 1830 at Agua Caliente before Juan J. Warner was granted the land which became Rancho San José del Valle. Warner Resort Company made the structure into a guest cottage.

These bells, cast in 1723 and 1767, were brought from Loreto, Baja California, in the early 1800's to call the Indian converts to church services at Santa Ysabel. They were stolen in 1926 and were never recovered.

14

Santa Ysabel Rancho

In the early 1800's Santa Ysabel Rancho was owned by the Catholic Church and administered by the padres of San Diego Mission, who grazed large numbers of cattle and sheep in the lush valleys during the summer when there was not enough grass to support their herds and flocks nearer the coast.

More than a century later it was still a beautiful mountain-and-valley ranch of about 13,000 acres, fifty miles northeast of San Diego on Highways 78 and 79.

Originally there were hundreds of Indians living in the area and they impressed the padres as being of more than average intelligence. The mission fathers constructed an adobe chapel in 1818. It is recorded that in 1822 there were several houses, a granary, a cemetery and about 450 Indian converts.

The first chapel collapsed and was replaced by a small wooden building. This burned many years later, to be replaced in 1924 by a more modern church. The chapel had two large bells obtained by the Indians from Rosario Mission in Baja California in the early 1800's. One bell was cast in 1723, the other in 1767, and both came from Loreto, Baja California.

After the collapse of the original chapel, the bells hung beside the road near a crude brush structure the Indians used as a place of worship. The bells were stolen in 1926 and were never recovered. The two bell clappers were found many years later, leading to the belief that the thieves had cut up the bells in the hope they might contain gold.

A part of one of the bells was recovered in 1966 although its whereabouts since 1926 has never been revealed.

In 1834 the California missions were forced to give up all their land holdings and for the next decade Santa Ysabel Rancho, named by the padres in honor of Saint Ysabel, or Elizabeth, was ownerless.

In 1844, Edward F. Stokes, an English merchant ship captain, and José Joaquín Ortega, his father-in-law, who had been administrator of San Diego Mission, applied for and received Santa Ysabel Rancho as a land grant from Gov. Manuel Micheltorena. The grant was for 17,719 acres.

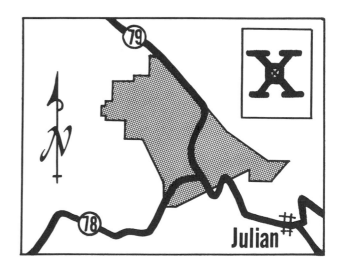

In 1843, Stokes and Ortega had been granted the Santa María Rancho, now the site of Ramona. Stokes had married Doña Refugio, the daughter of Ortega.

Stokes and Ortega stocked the Santa Ysabel with cattle and sheep, operating it in conjunction with the Santa María. They believed the two ranchos joined, but later surveys showed the boundaries were several miles apart.

When Gen. Stephen W. Kearny and his small American force crossed the desert in 1846, on their way to San Diego, they stopped at Rancho San José del Valle, now Warner Springs.

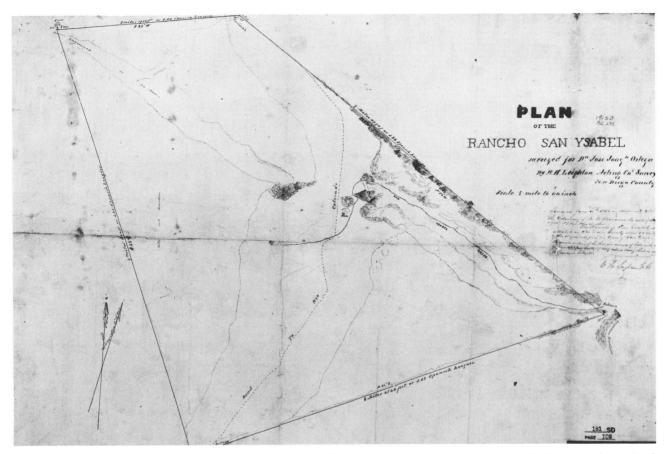

Don José Joaquín Ortega was the claimant before the U.S. Land Commission for Santa Ysabel Rancho, which he owned with his son-in-law, Capt. Edward Stokes. This diseño *maps boundaries of the 17,719-acre grant.*

There Kearny was given supplies, but his men and horses were in such poor condition the general decided to send a courier to San Diego to ask Commodore Stockton for reinforcements. He summoned Stokes from Santa Ysabel Rancho; the Englishman proclaimed himself a neutral but agreed to carry the message.

Richard F. Pourade in his book, *The Silver Dons*, described Stokes' arrival in San Diego and subsequent events leading up to the Battle of San Pasqual:

"At San Diego, on December 3, a strange courier arrived with a message for Commodore Stockton. He was clad in a black velvet English hunting coat, and wore long, clanking spurs. He was Edward Stokes, the English sea captain and rancher from Santa Ysabel.

"He brought a message reporting the arrival of General Kearny at Warner's Pass. The same evening, at 8 o'clock, Captain Gillespie left the pueblo with a force consisting of Capt. Samuel Gibson's Company of Mounted Riflemen, volunteers twenty-seven strong, and Lieut. Edward F. Beale of the USS *Congress*, with a four-pounder known as the Sutter gun, and passed Midshipman James M. Duncan with ten carbineers....

"From the large Pico house, Mariquita, sister of Andrés Pico, watched the men file out in the cold, sharp night and take the padre road up Mission Valley in the direction of El Cajon. She scribbled a warning note and sent it to her brother. The word of the arrival of new American forces in California also passed from Indian to Indian from the Colorado River to Soledad Valley, where Pico was encamped with his Californios."

When padres from the San Diego Mission explored the Santa Ysabel area they were much impressed by the intelligence of the Indians living there. This chapel was built in 1818 to serve the large number of converts.

Beautiful little church at Santa Ysabel was the third built on the rancho. The first, constructed of adobe, collapsed and was replaced by a wooden structure, which burned. The masonry chapel was constructed in 1924.

Aerial view shows Santa Ysabel Rancho. Range cattle still grazed in the wide valley and surrounding hills as they did more than a century ago, but a dairy had been added. The highway shown at right leads to Julian.

Thus was the stage set for Battle of San Pasqual.

The troops from San Diego met Kearny's men on the road between Santa Ysabel Rancho and Santa María Rancho, and together they continued on to where the Californios awaited them at San Pasqual.

In 1968 hundreds of beef cattle grazed on the hills and in the valleys of Santa Ysabel Rancho, just as in the days of the rancheros. But something new had been added. Several hundred purebred milk cows were on this modern-day rancho, and tanker trucks took the milk daily to San Diego.

In the days of the Dons, despite the large number of cattle, there was very little milk available. It was said that it took three men to milk a cow after she was roped and thrown to the ground—one to hold her head, another to keep the hungry calf away and

to keep the cow from kicking, and a third to do the milking.

The modern-day ranch had as its owner the Santa Ysabel Ranch, Inc., of which Victor Cauzza, ranch superintendent, was president, Charles Forward, vice president, and Orville Cumming, San Diego County cattleman, secretary-treasurer.

Some of the ranch employes were from the 15,000-acre Indian reservation which adjoins the ranch on the northwest. Steve Ponchetti was the chief, or spokesman, for the tribe. His ancestors lived in the Santa Ysabel area and he grew up there. The reservation was created by an act signed by President Grant in 1875.

No trace remained in 1968 of any early-day adobe houses on the Santa Ysabel.

60

15

Pauma Rancho and Cuca Rancho

The 13,309-acre Pauma Rancho was about midway between Rancho Santa Margarita y las Flores, now Camp Pendleton, and Rancho San José del Valle, Warner Springs, in northern San Diego County.

Pauma's little neighbor, Cuca Rancho, 2,174 acres, was about a mile to the east.

Pauma Rancho was granted to José Antonio Serrano by Gov. Manuel Micheltorena in 1844. He built an adobe home and stocked the rancho with cattle and horses.

Serrano got along well with the Indians in the area, and his herds thrived on the well-watered lands of the valley and on the surrounding hillsides.

In 1846 came an Indian attack on Don José's home which was to mark Pauma Rancho for a place in history.

Serrano was a staunch supporter of the Pico brothers in their resistance to the American advance into California. He rode with Gen. Andrés Pico at the Battle of San Pasqual, then fled back to his rancho when the Pico forces scattered. Some of his ranchero friends, fearing retaliation from the Americans, fled with him to isolated Pauma Rancho.

Don José had received word that his wife and small children had gone to Pala to stay with friends.

He rode to a nearby Indian village to get supplies for his companions; there he overheard two Indian women talking about an impending raid on his rancho. Returning to the Pauma, he told his friends, but they were well armed and scoffed at the warning.

About sundown, Serrano saddled his horse for the ride to Pala to join his family. He was accompanied by his 14-year-old son Jesús, and José Aguilar, his brother-in-law.

There were ten men and a boy asleep in the Serrano ranchhouse that cold December night when there came a knock on the door. One of the rancheros, José María Alvarado, owner of Los Vallecitos de San Marcos Rancho, called out. The familiar voice of Manuelito Cota, a Luiseño Indian chief who had been friendly with the Californios, answered and the door was unbarred.

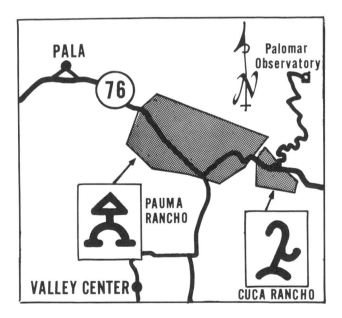

Immediately a score of Indians rushed in and quickly overpowered the rancheros. They were stripped of most of their clothing, tied on the backs of horses and taken to an Indian village at what is now Warner Springs.

Details of what occurred next are told graphically by Richard F. Pourade in his book, *The Silver Dons*:

"The captured men were first put on exhibition at

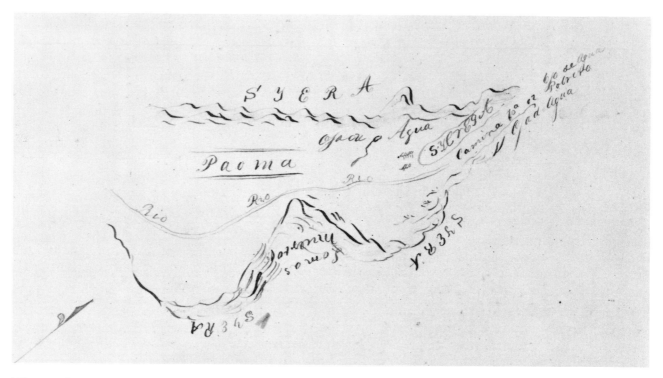

The top diseño *supported the claim of José A. Serrano to Pauma Rancho, granted to him in 1844. María Juana de Los Angeles presented the map below to the U.S. Land Commission in her claim for Cuca Rancho.*

Pauma Valley in 1968 bore little resemblance to the days when José Antonio Serrano raised cattle in the area. There were many estates of a few acres, scores of small ranches and groves, a golf course and schools.

Agua Caliente for the benefit of the Cupeños at Warner's, the Cahuillas of the eastern mountain and desert areas, and the Luiseños of the San Luis Rey Mission lands.

"Manuelito, in a change of heart, wanted to set the captives free. His companion, Pablo Apis, was against it. Here the story becomes more murky, obscured by legend and old hates. Counsel was sought from two persons, an American, Bill Marshall, the sea-faring deserter of Warner's, and a Mexican renegade named Yguera who had married a Cupeño woman. It was Marshall who is believed to have influenced the Luiseños to kill their captives, by arguing that the American conquerers would be greatly pleased.

"There are two versions of the manner of their deaths. One is that they were forced to stand and then were shot full of arrows. The other is that they were lanced to death with spears heated in the fire.

"The story is told that Santiago Alipás, only thirteen years old, alone remained calm in the face of death, and was rewarded with execution by gunfire. The bodies were piled in a heap and the Indians danced around them all night."

Besides the boy and Alvarado, those killed were: Manuel Serrano, brother of Don José; Ramón Aguilar, Francisco Basualdo, a relative of Pío Pico; Santiago Osuna, José López, Estaquio Ruiz, Juan de la Cruz, a man named Domínguez and another man from New Mexico whose name was not recorded.

Don José and his brother-in-law, when they learned of the kidnapping, picked up the trail and followed it to Agua Caliente, from where they sent an appeal to Bill Williams at Santa Ysabel, and the chief of the Santa Ysabel Indians, Ignacio.

Williams sent an Indian with an offer of ransom for the men, and when that failed he went to the Indian camp himself. There he saw the captives lying bound on the ground. He was warned to leave or be killed himself.

The massacre took place that night.

A short time later, Gen. José María Flores dispatched seventeen men from his troops in the north to take revenge on the Luiseño band responsible for the massacre. The men were joined by a band of Cahuillas led by José Antonio. The combined force ambushed a party of Luiseños near Aguanga, killing many. The rest were taken prisoner and turned over to José Antonio. He ordered them all slaughtered, including women and children.

Much of Pauma, an Indian word meaning "I bring water," later was cut up into scores of small citrus groves. Also there were many estates covering a few acres each, a large golf course, schools and stores in the beautiful valley at the base of Palomar Mountain. The big cattle ranch of a century ago had disappeared.

Arthur L. Cook was the owner in 1968 of the Serrano adobe where the rancheros were captured.

A previous owner had added several rooms and Cook did some remodeling. The house was a few hundred feet off Highway 76.

Adobe walls of the original house were twenty-four inches thick. The doorway through which the Indians attacked more than a century ago opened into a room built later. Its adobe walls were only a foot thick. Whether Don José or a later owner added this room is not known.

Cook purchased the house and fifty acres of land in 1955. He found many metates, Indian grinding stones, on his land and once uncovered a small brass altar bell stamped with the year 1878.

Cuca Rancho was granted to María Juana de Los Angeles by Gov. Pío Pico in 1845. She married a man named Sobernes and one of their daughters married Grigorio Trujillo. A few of the Trujillo descendants retained small parcels of land in the area.

Enos T. Mendenhall and his family came to San Diego in 1869. He and his sons, George, Sylvester and Richard, homesteaded on Palomar Mountain

The Serrano ranchhouse on Pauma Rancho in 1968, after several rooms had been added. This was the scene of an Indian attack in 1846; ten rancheros and a boy were kidnapped, taken to Agua Caliente and murdered.

and began raising cattle. In 1895 they purchased Cuca Rancho for winter range.

Manchester Boddy, Los Angeles newspaper publisher, purchased Cuca in 1954. He later sold the property to a group which included Col. Irving Salomon of San Diego.

In 1960, John B. Kilroy of Newport Beach purchased the rancho, which by then totaled only 1,800 acres. He leased the land to A. F. Alford Sr. and his son, Mesa Grande cattlemen.

Cuca, named for a root used as a substitute for coffee, managed to evade the inexorable march of civilization which swallowed up many of the early-day ranchos. Cuca in 1968 was still a cattle ranch.

16

Cañada de San Vicente Rancho

Don Juan Bautista López was the first owner of Cañada de San Vicente Rancho, a 13,316-acre irregular-shaped tract of well-watered valleys and canyons and wooded hills south and slightly east of Ramona.

The rancho, granted to him by Gov. Pío Pico in 1845, was known also as Cañada de San Vicente y Mesa del Padre Barona. The southern part of the tract, later to become the Barona Indian Reservation, was named for a San Diego Mission priest, Father Josef Barona, who ministered to the Indians in the area in the early years of the 1880's.

Early-day records reveal little about Don Juan. It is known that he built an adobe home in Old Town near that of his friend, Don Santiago Arguello. The latter, who was *alcalde* in 1836, was granted the huge Rancho de la Misión San Diego de Alcalá in 1846.

López and his wife, Doña María Josefa, built an adobe home on the rancho and stocked the land with horses and cattle, but no trace of the house remained in 1968.

In 1850 he deeded the property to Don Domingo Yorba, member of a prominent California family. Don Juan, who could not write, made his mark on

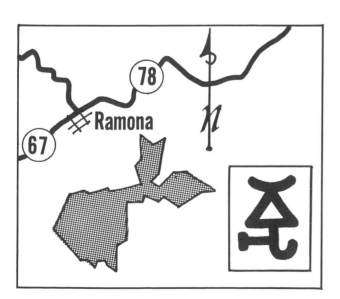

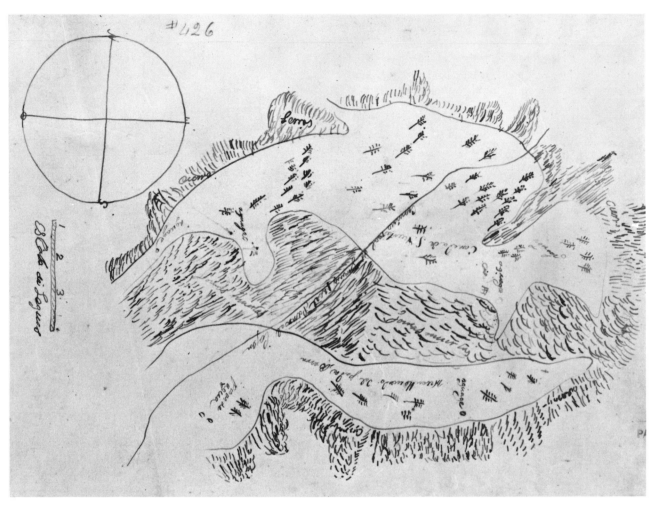

Don Domingo Yorba was the second owner of Cañada de San Vicente Rancho. He bought the property from Juan Bautista López in 1850. This diseño *supported claim of Don Domingo before the U.S. Land Commission.*

the deed, which specified that he and his wife were to receive $2,000, and Yorba was to feed, clothe and provide a house for López and his wife as long as they lived.

The Yorba family continued to raise horses and cattle on the rancho, and in 1852 Don Domingo filed a claim for the property with the U.S. Land Commission; his title was confirmed two years later.

In 1886 the rancho was sold to Charles V. Howard for $8,000. A year later it was sold again, this time for $20,000, and the property was cut up into many tracts of various sizes.

A few large ranches and a number of small ones remained. The largest single tract, about 4,000 acres, is the Barona Indian Reservation. It was purchased in 1933 by the United States government as a home for the Indians who were displaced when El Capitan Dam and Reservoir were built.

The Indians' neat little homes were built along Wildcat Canyon Road northeast of Lakeside. They had a few horses and cattle; tractors were used to till their farms and trucks took their crops to market.

Beside the road is the Assumption Church, Barona Mission. In the churchyard a pole framework was built, which the Indians covered with tree branches for use during *fiestas*.

There were still cattle ranches on the old land grant in 1968. One was owned by James Barnett of

Assumption Church, Barona Mission, where in 1968 Sunday services were held for the Indians of Barona Reservation. Homes of the Indians were near by. Area originally was part of the Cañada de San Vicente Rancho.

San Marino. He was a grandson of Augustus Barnett, who about 1880 built a large U-shaped adobe home on a little hill a quarter mile off San Vicente Road.

Charles Hughes had nearly 3,000 acres which he leased to D. E. Scarbery. The land formerly was owned by Mr. and Mrs. Scarbery.

Mrs. Scarbery's father, J. W. Mykrantz. purchased 7,000 acres of the old land grant in 1921. He constructed seven concrete dams in canyons on the property between 1922 and 1925, storing a considerable amount of water for irrigation. In the floods of 1927 all were washed out. One of the dams, which was nearly 300 feet long, was alongside San Vicente Road.

When this dam went out the homes of four families were carried away, including that of the Mykrantzes. Mrs. Scarbery recalled that canned goods and other objects from the houses were washed down the creek and some were found as far away as Lakeside.

Down through the years, several mining operations were started on the old rancho; small amounts of gold, silver and copper were found. All mining ceased about 1930.

Another tract of several thousand acres was the Monte Vista Ranch, once called the Angora goat ranch. The goats thrived but the project was a failure because the heavy brush in the area tore the animals' long hair and even their skins. The land later was purchased by Harry L. Summers, president of Rancho Bernardo, Inc.

Polled Hereford cattle graze on 3,000-acre ranch, the largest tract remaining in 1968 of what once was a 13,316-acre Mexican land grant. Most of the original acreage was sold for country homes and small ranches.

17

Guajome Rancho

The huge and beautiful ranchhouse at Guajome Rancho was one of the grandest of the homes from which the Dons of San Diego County ruled their vast domains a century ago.

In 1968 the big house—some of its adobe walls were four feet thick—still sat in lonely grandeur on a little hill just north of Vista's city limits.

Gone were the days when its twenty rooms resounded with children's laughter, when the Don's smaller youngsters played in the spacious patio and the older ones raced their ponies over the hills, and neighboring rancheros and their families were guests at week-long *fiestas*.

Gone were the many *vaqueros* who rounded up and branded the Don's cattle, the multitude of Indian servants who cooked, washed clothes, kept the house spotless, and the laborers who tended the vegetable gardens and made adobe bricks for the new barns, walls and corrals the Don was continually building.

This once magnificent Mexican-type adobe home was beginning to show the ravages of time. It was still beautiful, but its owner, Mrs. Ida Richardson, and her son, Earl Richardson, did not have the time nor the help needed to keep the big house in the condition it once was.

Guajome Rancho was a 2,219-acre Mexican land grant given by Gov. Pío Pico in 1845 to two Indian brothers, Andrés and José Manuel. Guajome is pronounced wah-ho'-may; it is an Indian word meaning "home of the frog." There were five ponds and lakes on the rancho.

A short time later the Indians sold the rancho to Abel Stearns, a Los Angeles business man, for $550.

About that time a young American Army lieutenant, Cave Johnson Couts, was projected upon the San Diego scene. He was a West Point graduate, born in Tennessee in 1821, a nephew of Cave Johnson, who became Secretary of the Treasury under President Polk.

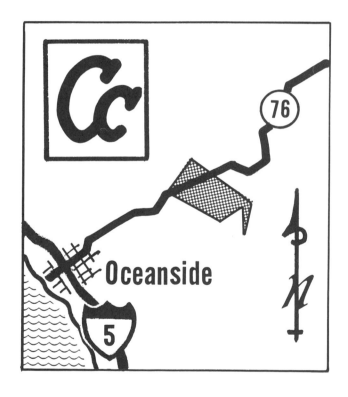

Cave Couts served on the frontier during the Mexican War and arrived in San Diego in 1848 with the 1st Dragoons. He served in San Diego, Los Angeles and San Luis Rey. In 1849 he was commissioned to survey and map San Diego's pueblo lands, and later he accompanied the Whipple expedition to establish the exact point of the confluence of the Gila and Colorado rivers. For a time during the days of the gold rush he operated a ferry near Ft. Yuma.

Early-day sketch shows the ranchhouse and corrals at Guajome Rancho. Near the windmill at center is the chapel built by Cave Couts in memory of his mother. A resident priest also tutored the children of the rancho.

He served as a member of the county's first grand jury and was a county judge for a short time.

In 1851 Couts married Doña Ysidora Bandini, daughter of one of San Diego's most prominent citizens, Don Juan Bandini. Another of Don Juan's daughters, Doña Arcadia, was married to Abel Stearns, and the latter presented Guajome Rancho to Cave Couts and his bride as a wedding gift. Six months later Couts resigned from the Army. Soon thereafter he was commissioned as a colonel and aide-de-camp on the staff of Gov. John Bigler.

Development of Guajome Rancho was a monumental task, but the Colonel, as he was known after receiving the governor's appointment, was determined not only to become a successful ranchero but to have the finest ranchhouse in the county.

When Couts first took over the property there were no buildings, and no trees were in the area he chose for his ranchhouse. He hauled a few boards from San Diego and cut poles in the riverbed two miles away; with this material he erected a shack in which he slept and cooked his meals.

Colonel Couts first recruited 300 Indians from the area as workmen. He had designed the twenty-room adobe home, with its huge patio, servants' quarters, barns, stables, sheds and corrals, but his laborers' knowledge of construction was limited. Some had worked at San Luis Rey Mission but the experience of the majority consisted only of making crude native huts of poles and tree branches. So the Colonel trained the best workmen as foremen and they in turn trained the others.

Adobe had to be dug from the ground and molded into bricks—thousands upon thousands of them—then baked in the sun. Huge timbers had to be hauled for miles, then hand-hewn for use as roof supports.

The work progressed slowly, for part of the Colonel's time had to be devoted to the raising of cattle, as it was through the sale of these animals that he was able to pay the not inconsiderable cost of building his huge home.

Years passed and the Guajome Rancho herds multiplied—Couts even trail-herded hundreds of cattle to San Francisco to get a better price for them.

Finally the ranchhouse was completed. There were twenty rooms in four wings built around a patio eighty by ninety feet. A fifth wing extended from the north side; it housed a huge bake-oven, the kitchen and quarters for the cooks.

A series of arches crossed the front of the house, partly enclosing the *galería*, or outside porch. A few hundred yards to the west was a small lake.

In the center of the patio was a fountain. An iron gate near the southeast corner led into a second patio, or outer court. Here was a large open fireplace and the carriage entrance. Along the eastern side was the carriage house and stables for the carriage

Guajome Rancho was a wedding gift when Cave Couts, an Army officer, married Ysidora Bandini.

horses; the northern wall housed a large blacksmith shop and a carpenter shop. A room on the west side contained a small store where rancho workers could purchase clothing and various other items. There also was a leather shop where shoes and boots were made as well as saddles and bridles.

A short distance south of the house Colonel Couts built a chapel, dedicating it to his mother. A plaque recorded that it was constructed in 1868 and rebuilt in 1924. There was a resident priest who not only said mass for members of the family and the rancho workers, but also tutored the ten Couts children.

While the Colonel was a good business man and well thought of in San Diego, he had a fiery temper and during the years had several clashes with the law. Richard F. Pourade in his book, *The Silver Dons*, related that Couts was indicted by the San Diego County Grand Jury twice in 1855, on charges of beating two Indians with a rawhide *reata*. One was a boy, and in his case Couts was acquitted on a charge of assault. In the other case, the Indian, named Halbani, died as a result of the beating and Couts was tried on a charge of manslaughter brought by the Grand Jury. Couts' attorney, O. S. Witherby, won a dismissal on the contention one of the grand jurors was an alien.

Strife between landowners and squatters rose in intensity in 1865, Pourade related. Couts was indicted on a charge that he and his brother had murdered four Indians and a Negro workman. Details are missing from old records, but Couts' attorney, who again was Witherby, obtained dismissal of the indictment, this time on the grounds the district attorney had not posted his bond of office.

Pourade also told of another indictment of Couts the following year. He was tried and acquitted of murdering one Juan Mendoza. The latter had worked for Couts as his *mayordomo*, after a reputed career as a badman in Sonora. Couts' defense was that he had discharged Mendoza, who then threatened to kill him on sight.

For months Couts stayed away from San Diego, while Mendoza, armed with a six-shooter and a knife, held forth at various bars and sent challenges to Couts.

Carriage entrance to second patio of Guajome Rancho is shown in this early-day sketch. The door at right opened into the main patio, around which the big adobe house was built. There was a fireplace near the door.

In time, Couts appeared in San Diego, reportedly on business. In the tradition of the Old West, either by design or by chance, they walked toward each other in the area of the Plaza.

Couts was carrying a shawl. He dropped it, to reveal a shotgun. Mendoza, according to witnesses, turned to flee and was struck with a blast from both barrels. He staggered into a heap of weeds and died.

Colonel Couts died in a room at the Horton House in San Diego in 1874. Cave Couts Jr. inherited the rancho and lived in the old ranchhouse until his death in 1943 at the age of eighty-seven. He had been married to Lilly Belle Clemons; they had a son, Cave III, who died in 1948 at the age of sixty-one. Colonel Couts, his son and grandson were buried in Calvary Cemetery in San Diego.

The rancho in 1968 totaled only about 600 acres. For years the Richardsons farmed most of the land,

employing a large number of field workers. Later they raised only cattle and leased additional range.

The big adobe home retained much of its early-day charm, but Mrs. Richardson feared its days were numbered. The rancho's location placed it directly in the path of surburban development. It was offered to the state as a park, but the expense involved in proposed development caused it to be refused.

Later a bill was introduced in Congress to create a national historic site of the rancho buildings. It was planned to purchase 360 acres of the original grant, to restore the ranchhouse and other buildings, and operate the rancho under the National Park Service. It was expected that a small herd of cattle and horses would be maintained, with Mexican and Indian *vaqueros* working and living on the rancho as they did more than a century ago.

18

Buena Vista Rancho

Most of the vast ranchos of the Dons in San Diego's back country in the 1800's were swallowed up in the march of progress.

A few remained intact as late as the 1960's, but most of the ranchos had fallen victim to the tremendous population growth in Southern California —cities and suburban developments occupied the hills and valleys where thousands of cattle once grazed.

Most of the adobe homes of the Dons also disappeared because of their owners' neglect. Some of the original ranchhouses were saved, with their two- to three-foot-thick walls incorporated into modern dwellings. But few of these remodeled homes bore much resemblance to the ranchhouses built by the Dons.

Buena Vista Rancho, which is translated as "good view," is no longer the large cattle ranch of a century ago. Its 1,184 acres now are part of the city of Vista. But its beautiful U-shaped adobe ranchhouse of twelve rooms, where once laughing, dark-eyed señoritas danced the *fandango* with the dashing sons of neighboring Dons, still stood in 1968 almost in the center of the city, its appearance little changed in more than 100 years.

The ranchhouse had many owners, but each had a love for the imposing structure, and made his

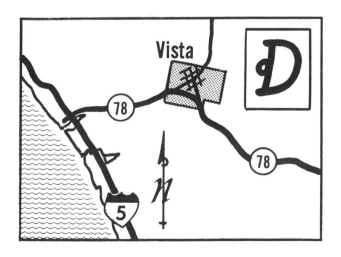

Sketch made in 1913 shows view of corredor, *or inside porch, and corner of patio at Buena Vista ranchhouse. Remodeled and modernized through the years, the large adobe home retained its Mexican style architecture.*

home there, protecting the ancient adobe from the attacks of time and the elements.

The rambling house was changed, of course. Modern plumbing, heating and lighting had been added, but the huge patio with its fountain and wishing well, its trees and shrubbery, were much the same as they were a century ago.

Buena Vista Rancho was once part of the vast grazing lands administered by the padres of San Luis Rey Mission. In 1845, Gov. Pío Pico granted the rancho to an Indian, Felipe Subria. After holding it only a few years he gave the property to his married daughter, Marie La Gradia Dunn.

The next owner was Jesús Machado, who was killed by Indians. The rancho passed to his son Luis, who began construction of the ranchhouse. The Lorenzo family then purchased the property, but soon sold it to Cave Johnson Couts, a former U. S. Army officer who owned two neighboring ranchos, the Guajome and Vallecitos de San Marcos.

Additional rooms were added by each successive owner. It was during the Couts period of ownership that Buena Vista Rancho was best known for the splendor of its social life.

Couts gave the rancho to his daughter, María Antonia, before her marriage to Judge Chalmers Scott. The couple moved to the rancho in 1879. Mrs. Scott's sister, Ysidora Forster Couts, who was heavily in debt, was given the rancho a few years later by the Scotts. She borrowed $8,500 on the property and then lost it through bank foreclosure.

Most of the land was sold off in small parcels and

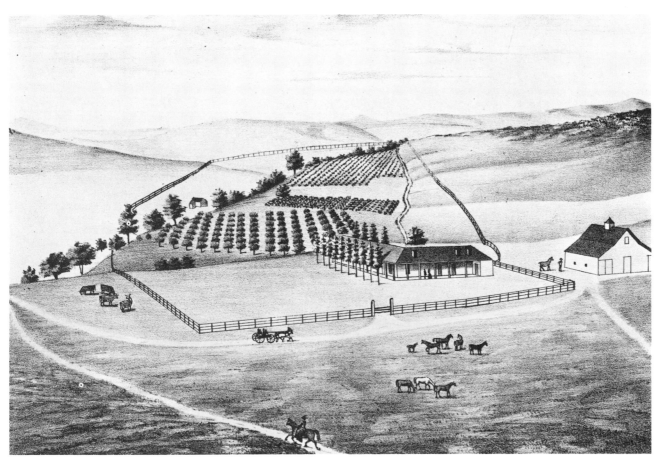

This is the way Buena Vista ranchhouse looked in 1879, when it was the home of Judge and Mrs. Chalmers Scott. The rancho was a gift to Mrs. Scott from her father, Cave Couts, who also owned the Guajome Rancho.

Polished tile floor and iron grillwork on the doors mark this corredor *in the patio of Buena Vista ranchhouse. The beautiful home—all that remained of the once-large rancho—had many owners down through the years.*

Buena Vista ranchhouse and its two-and-a-half-acre site were surrounded by modern-day town of Vista. There was a fountain in the center of the gracious patio and a wall of adobe and stone encircled the grounds.

in the early 1920's only fifty-one acres remained. Mr. and Mrs. Jack Knight bought the property and restored the run-down ranchhouse. In 1931 they sold the place to Mr. and Mrs. Harry Pollard of Hollywood, who also did much to improve the old house. Twenty years later the ranchhouse and eight and one-half acres were sold to Mr. and Mrs. Fredrick Reid of Las Vegas. The next owners were Dr. and Mrs. Walter J. Weil.

Dr. Weil was an ophthamologist; he and Mrs. Weil divided their time between Vista and Los Angeles.

The Weils furnished the old ranchhouse in the Mexican-Spanish style. Many large oil paintings decorated the plastered walls. Chandeliers were huge and were of wrought iron; the doors and windows had ornate iron gratings. Some of the floors were of polished eight-inch tiles, others were hardwood. The ceilings were beamed.

The ranchhouse occupied a two-and-one-fourth-acre site near the center of Vista. Yet when one walked through the gate in the heavy stone wall into the patio he seemed suddenly transported back a hundred years. All was quiet and peaceful; traffic noises were muted and the hustle and bustle of the city seemed far away.

19

Cuyamaca Rancho

Most of San Diego County's great land-grant ranchos were valuable for their grazing lands and the thousands of cattle and horses that ranged the fenceless acres.

Cuyamaca is an Indian word meaning "rain above." Cuyamaca Rancho, 35,501 acres of mountain timber land granted to Agustín Olvera by Gov. Pío Pico in 1845, was the exception. There were many fertile valleys on the vast rancho, but Olvera was not a ranchero and he had no interest in raising cattle.

No one knows today just why Olvera wanted such a large grant—probably he saw possibilities in marketing the timber on the forested slopes. Some think that, with Governor Pico passing out grants with a lavish hand during the last days of his regime, Olvera decided he too might as well claim a huge rancho. The fact that his wife, the former Concepción Arguello, was a niece of the governor undoubtedly helped to cut through the red tape in acquiring the land.

Olvera's petition for the grant was not accompanied by the usual maps and descriptions of boundaries. The grant specified that he was to appear before José A. Estudillo, justice of the peace in San Diego, and that the rancho was to be measured and maps made. Estudillo reported later that because of

heavy rains, roads to the mountains were impassable; he later estimated from a map made by Olvera that the rancho contained eight square leagues.

In 1854 Olvera's claim before the U.S. Land Commission for a patent was rejected, but the district court in 1858 confirmed the grant.

Olvera was born in Mexico City in 1818 and came to Los Angeles in 1834. He held various political offices there, including county judge and member of the state Assembly. Olvera Street in Los Angeles was named for him.

Don Agustín never built a home on Cuyamaca Rancho and only visited it occasionally. In about 1848 he sent a representative, Cesario Walker, to construct a water sawmill on the rancho and begin lumbering operations. There was trouble with the Indians, who had several rancherías in the area, and Walker and his men fled.

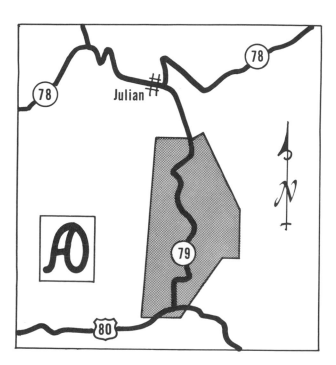

There were many lush meadows on the grant and Don Agustín permitted rancheros for many miles around to graze cattle and horses there in the summer months.

Olvera also seemingly had no objection to squat-

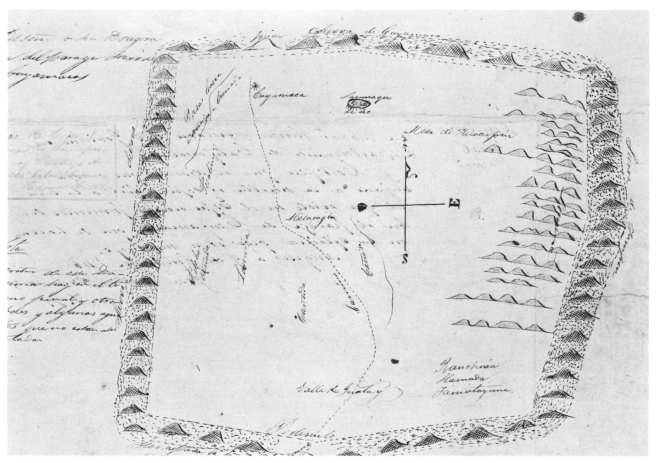

Agustín Olvera was the grantee of Cuyamaca Rancho in 1845 and the claimant to the 35,501-acre tract of timbered mountain land before the U.S. Land Commission. This is the map he presented to back his claim.

ters on his land, for in 1857, James R. Lassator, who operated a store and hay station for travelers at Vallecito, was allowed to build a stone house in what later became Green Valley, near Highway 79. Lassator cut wild hay in the nearby meadows, and sledded it down to his desert station. His place at Cuyamaca also was a rest stop for the Jackass Mail route which followed an old Indian trail from Vallecitos up Oriflamme Canyon to Cuyamaca, thence to Guatay and San Diego.

Olvera sold Cuyamaca Rancho in 1869 to Robert Allison, Isaac Hartman, Juan Luco and John Treat. A year later gold was discovered on the rancho and also a few miles north in the Julian area. William Skidmore, while trailing a stray mule near the southern edge of Cuyamaca Lake, detected gold in a small quartz ledge. With his three sons and son-in-law he filed a claim, calling his mine the Stonewall Jackson, after the Civil War general. They later sold out to Charles and George Hensley and Almon P. Frary.

Then followed a long lawsuit filed by the new owners of the rancho, who claimed that the grant's boundaries took in the Julian gold diggings, and that they were entitled to a royalty on each ton of gold mined. The miners won the suit, with the northern boundary of the rancho set about four and one-half miles south of Julian. Don Agustín received the patent, signed by President U. S. Grant in 1874, and turned it over to the owners.

The Stonewall Mine, as the name was shortened, changed ownership several times until, in 1886,

The greater part of Cuyamaca Rancho was purchased as a state park in 1933. This photo shows Cuyamaca Lake at right center of the large snow-covered valley and Sunrise Highway to Laguna Mountain at left center.

The old Stonewall Mine on Cuyamaca Rancho was abandoned after the bursting of the gold bubble in 1893. More than two million dollars' worth of the precious metal had been taken out before the mine was closed.

John Treat owned this farm in a valley in Cuyamaca Rancho in 1869. With three partners he had bought the rancho from Agustín Olvera. Gold was discovered there the following year by a man who was trailing a mule.

Robert W. Waterman bought it and 26,000 acres of the rancho. The following year he was elected governor of California. Waterman's son, Waldo, operated the Stonewall, sinking a second shaft to a depth of 630 feet. Drifts totaled 2,700 feet on six levels; sixty-five men worked underground and eight in the mill between 1888 and 1891 when the mine produced more than $900,000 in gold.

A settlement grew up around the mine, with many small houses, a hotel and a post office.

The gold bubble burst in 1893 when the accessible ore pinched out at the Stonewall, but not until after about two million dollars in gold had been taken out. The Sather Banking Co. of San Francisco took over the property to process mill tailings.

Col. A. G. Gassen bought the rancho and mine site in 1917, selling the property six years later to Ralph M. Dyar, who constructed a large stone ranchhouse on the property. In the building he uti-

lized some of the stones used in the Lassator house and many of the timbers taken from the mine buildings.

In March of 1933 Dyar sold 20,735 acres of the rancho to the state for about $125,000—half of the assessed valuation of the land—and Cuyamaca Rancho State Park was created.

Cuyamaca Lake was owned by the Helix Irrigation Co. In 1968 it covered about 100 surface acres and was twenty-five feet deep at the dam. The district leased the lake for twenty years to the Cuyamaca Recreation & Park District.

The Sawday-Cumming cattle interests had 2,000 acres of grazing land north of the lake.

None of the buildings nor machinery remained at the old Stonewall Mine. Many of the ore cars and other relics were rolled down the mine's open shaft before the park was created, and the buildings were sold for scrap to a Los Angeles wrecking company.

20

El Cajón Rancho and Rancho de la Cañada de los Coches

Huge El Cajón Rancho, the third largest land grant in San Diego County, is gone with the years—no trace remains of the 48,799-acre cattle ranch where the padres from San Diego Mission grazed their herds and Indian converts cultivated vineyards and corn fields more than a century ago.

El Cajón is translated as "the box," though there has been historic reference to its meaning as "the pass between two hills."

By contrast, California's smallest land grant, Rancho de la Cañada de los Coches, or "glen of the hogs," containing twenty-eight and one-third acres, was completely surrounded by El Cajón Rancho and it retained its identity for more than 100 years. It was reduced in size, however, and totaled only eleven and one-half acres.

The vast rancho of the padres became the site of El Cajon, Lakeside, Santee, Bostonia and Flinn Springs. Original boundaries of the rancho, roughly, were La Mesa on the west, Mt. Helix on the south, Camp Elliott on the north and El Monte Park on the east.

Los Coches is near Johnstown, a few miles north-

east of El Cajon on old Highway 80. A historic marker contributed by the Native Sons of the Golden West was placed at the turnoff to the rancho.

Before secularization of the California missions in 1834 the Church operated El Cajón Rancho, also known as Santa Mónica Rancho, and there was no Los Coches. For the next ten years the rancho was virtually ownerless, although some of the mission cattle still were allowed to graze there.

Rancho de la Cañada de los Coches was the first of the two to be granted to private ownership. Gov. Manuel Micheltorena made the grant in 1843 to Doña Apolinaria Lorenzana, who also was grantee of Jamacha Rancho. Doña Apolinaria was called La Beata, a title given women who were charitable and devout. She was one of eight orphans brought from Mexico in the early 1800's.

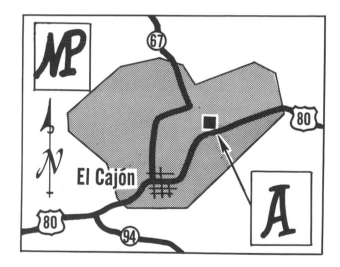

Los Coches had been used by the padres for years as a grazing ground for the mission's hogs. Records are vague, but it is believed the grant was made to Doña Apolinaria so this use of the land could be assured in the future.

El Cajón Rancho, aside from its size, was one of the most desirable ranchos in San Diego County. It was granted in 1845 to Doña María Antonia Estudillo de Pedrorena. She was the daughter of Don José Antonio Estudillo and the wife of Don Miguel de Pedrorena. Don José was the *alcalde* of San Diego. He built Casa de Estudillo, later known as

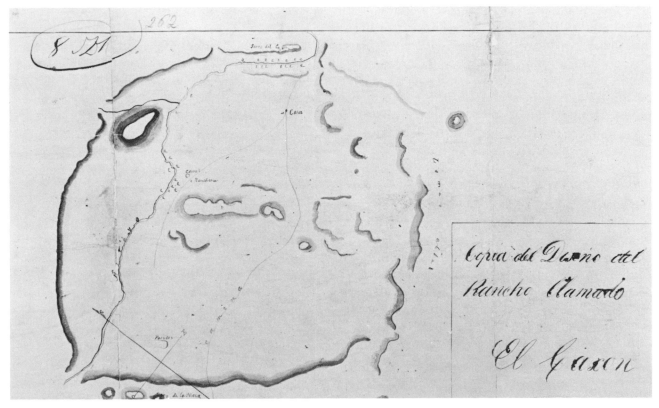

Don Miguel de Pedrorena and his wife, Doña María, owned El Cajón Rancho, but he died in 1850 before obtaining a U.S. deed to the land grant. T. W. Sutherland, a San Diego attorney, filed this diseño *for the heirs.*

Ramona's Marriage Place in Old Town. He also was owner of Janal Rancho.

The Pedrorena family built a large adobe home near what later was the center of Lakeside, and a smaller house near the eastern end of Mission Gorge. No trace remained in 1968 of either house.

Don Miguel first came to San Diego from Peru in 1837 as supercargo, or business agent, of the brig *Delmire*, of which he was part owner. He became a merchant and importer and was appointed collector of customs and harbor master in 1847. He also served as justice of the peace for a time. During the Mexican War he supported the American side and was captain of a cavalry troop.

Richard F. Pourade in his book, *The Silver Dons*, relates one story of Pedrorena's courage.

The captain, in full uniform, was escorting Doña Felipa Marrón to her Old Town residence from the nearby home of Doña María Ybañes when a rifle-man opened fire. Two bullets whizzed close to Pedrorena's head. The captain took off his hat and waved it politely at the rifleman.

The man who did the shooting was Don José María Orozco, owner of Guejito Rancho, who sided with the Mexican forces. Pedrorena seemed to bear him no ill will; Orozco explained he merely wanted to see if he "could make Miguel run."

Pedrorena died in 1850 and was buried in Old Town. His heirs were a son, Miguel Jr., and three daughters, Ysabel, Victoria and Elena. The U. S. Land Commission issued a patent to them for El Cajón Rancho in 1876.

Miguel Jr. had married Nellie Burton, daughter of Gen. H. S. Burton of the U. S. Army.

During the Civil War the Pedrorenas began to dispose of their land little by little. In 1868, Isaac Lankershim, a San Francisco capitalist, purchased the largest section of the remaining land for less than one dollar an acre. The following year most of the valley was opened to settlement.

Amaziah L. Knox, a New Englander whom Lankershim met in San Francisco, was employed to plant a large acreage in the valley to wheat and also to manage the Lankershim holdings. Knox later opened a tavern at what became Magnolia and Main streets in El Cajon, and when a post office was opened in 1878 he became the postmaster.

Maj. Levi Chase and A. T. Christian planted citrus groves in the valley. A group of Boston investors purchased a large tract in the north central section in 1886 and planted many acres of vineyards in what is now Bostonia.

For many years El Cajon Valley was an area of small citrus ranches and vineyards, but the tremendous population growth saw the passing of practically all of these. El Cajon, Lakeside and Santee became prosperous communities.

The population boom had little effect on Rancho de la Cañada de los Coches. In 1968 the little rancho was owned by Mr. and Mrs. Daniel E. Hughes, who lived in what was known as the Windmill House. There were two other cottages on the property and an antique shop.

The Windmill House was built about 1925 by Wilkins Wheatley, the last previous owner. The windmill's huge blades pumped water into a 3,000-gallon tank and also turned a generator which provided electricity for the rancho.

The first owner of Los Coches, Doña Apolinaria, raised hogs for the mission fathers for several years, then turned the property over to Fr. Anacleto Lestrade of Los Angeles. He in turn deeded the rancho to Thaddius Amat, bishop of Los Angeles and Monterey. The latter sold the property to Doña Perfecta Espinosa de Ames for $1,000. The sale took place in 1874, but Doña Perfecta and her husband, Jesse

Sketch shows Knox Station, early-day stagecoach stop and farm in El Cajon. The owner, Amaziah L. Knox, managed the huge Lankershim holdings in the valley and was appointed the town's first postmaster in 1878.

El Cajon was a sleepy little town in the 1880's, as this street scene of the business section shows. The largest section of El Cajón Rancho was sold in 1868 to Isaac Lankershim at a price of less than one dollar an acre.

More than a century ago the Pedrorena family raised thousands of cattle on the land which became the site of the city of El Cajon. The rancho once was used to graze the large mission herds. This view is from Mt. Helix.

TOWN RESIDENCE OF MAJ. CHASE.

Maj. Levi Chase developed a large section of the southern part of El Cajón Rancho before the turn of the century. Early-day sketch shows his country home, Cajón Villa, with farm buildings, orchard and vineyard.

Julian Ames, had operated the rancho since 1859. Ames had been an otter hunter and a soldier, and had held minor political offices in San Diego.

Ames developed the rancho extensively, constructing a small grain mill and a blacksmith shop. He also had several hundred cattle, which he grazed on El Cajón Rancho. He died in 1866. His widow eventually lost the property, which had been heavily mortgaged.

During the Ames ownership his adobe house was a stage stop on the San Diego-Julian route. In time the house disappeared.

L. V. Hoover was the next owner; he sold the property to Wheatley in 1925.

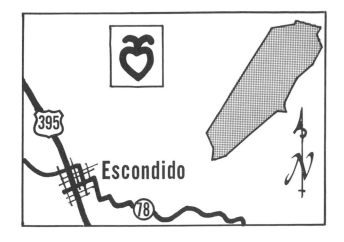

21

Rancho Guejito
y Cañada de Palomía

View of peaceful Guejito Valley is shown through window of the only house remaining on the rancho.

Down through the years, hundreds of thousands of cattle and horses have grazed the hills and valleys of huge Rancho Guejito y Cañada de Palomía near Lake Wohlford, northeast of Escondido.

In the days when the Dons held feudal sway over vast cattle ranches in San Diego County, the Guejito was host at countless *fiestas*, and neighbors for sixty miles around came on horseback or in crude ox-drawn *carretas* for merrymaking that continued sometimes for several days.

In 1968 an adobe ranchhouse—nine rooms, with a large attic and cellar—sat in decaying grandeur on a little rise overlooking a tree-lined valley. Its windows were without glass, part of its wooden roof had collapsed, and its thick adobe walls were crumbling. A hundred feet north of the house was a long, low adobe building which once was a winery. Its roof also had fallen in, leaving the walls unprotected from winter rains.

Rancho Guejito, pronounced way-hee'-toe, was granted to José María Orozco by Gov. Manuel Micheltorena in 1845. Guejito is translated as "small pebbles." Cañada de Palomía, meaning "glen of the small pigeon," was later dropped from the rancho name.

G. W. Hamley was the second owner of Rancho Guejito y Cañada de Palomía. This diseño *supported his claim before the U.S. Land Commission. Later owners added about 10,000 acres of adjoining land to original rancho.*

In the last century the 13,298-acre rancho had many owners, but always it had been a cattle ranch. One owner, however, planted a vineyard and constructed the winery. The rancho also increased in size, to about 23,000 acres.

Orozco, the first owner, had been a justice of the peace and collector of customs at San Diego. The next owner of the rancho was Capt. George W. Hamley, commander of the ship *Stonington*. Among other owners through the years of the early 1900's were Jacob Gruendike and Jean Cazaurang. Gru-

endike was a financier and land owner and was president of the Bank of Southern California in San Diego, which became the First National Bank, and was president of an Escondido Bank.

Cazaurang was well remembered by many modern-day cattlemen and ranchers. One of these was J. C. La Force. La Force recalled that Cazaurang was a red-haired Frenchman, quick-tempered but also kind-hearted. He had married a wealthy widow and with her funds purchased the Guejito, and later, a ranch in Nevada. After her death Cazaurang remarried, but did not get along too well with his second wife; she liked to entertain at dances and parties while he preferred a more quiet life.

Cazaurang constructed the adobe house in the early 1900's; in 1968 nothing remained of the ranch-house built by the first owner.

Cazaurang and his wife separated, and in 1929 the fiery-tempered rancher was shot and killed in a fight with a cowboy in Nevada. His estate was heavily mortgaged and its settlement left little for his widow, who died a few years later, almost penniless.

Charles L. Powell, wealthy construction engineer in Los Angeles, purchased the rancho in 1939 and stocked it with nearly 2,000 head of cattle. He repaired and modernized the Cazaurang adobe and installed a small electric light plant. Powell died in 1959.

The Guejito in 1968 was owned by the C. L. Powell estate but was leased to Orville A. Cumming and Russell Peavey, modern-day cattle ranchers.

This beautiful valley was the main part of the 13,298-acre Rancho Guejito y Cañada de Palomía. Cattle still grazed there in 1968 as they did in the days it was owned by José María Orozco more than a century ago.

22

Rancho de la Nación

The names of two men stand out in the history of Rancho de la Nación, the 26,631-acre Mexican land grant which became the site of two cities, National City and Chula Vista, as well as Bonita and Sunnyside.

They were Don Juan (John) Forster, who received the land grant in 1845 from his brother-in-law, Gov. Pío Pico, and Frank A. Kimball, who with his brothers, Warren and Levi, took the lead in developing the area in the late 1800's.

Originally the rancho was a grazing ground for the San Diego Mission herds and was called La Purísima, or "the most pure." It was taken over by the military in 1795; soldiers from the Presidio grazed their horses and a few cattle there. The military renamed it El Rancho del Rey, or the King's Ranch. The name was changed to Rancho de la Nación, or National Ranch, when Forster received the grant.

Forster, or Don Juan, as he was called, was born in Liverpool, England, in 1815. An uncle who had become wealthy as a merchant ship captain asked John's father to "lend me one of your seven sons." Young John was chosen, beginning the career which was to lead him to wealth as an importer and merchant, and finally to becoming one of the largest landowners in San Diego County.

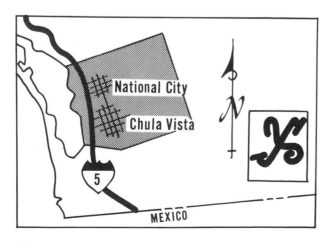

Forster first came to San Diego from Guaymas, Mexico, in 1833, bringing $50,000 worth of goods imported from China. These he sold in San Diego and Los Angeles, and returned to Guaymas by ship. Then he decided to return to San Diego, and rode horseback the entire distance.

He became prominent politically and married Doña Ysidora Pico, sister of Pío and Andrés Pico. Don Juan died in 1882; little of his fortune was left despite his once large land holdings, which had included San Felipe Rancho and Rancho Santa Margarita y las Flores, as well as Rancho de la Nación.

Francois Louis Pioche and J. B. Bayerque, San Francisco bankers, purchased Rancho de la Nación from Forster in 1856.

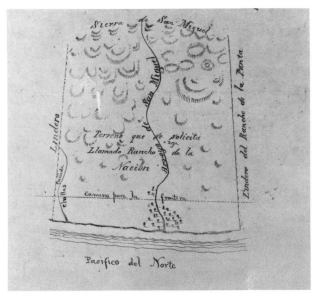

Don Juan Forster was grantee of Rancho de la Nación in 1845. This map supported his title claim.

In the 1860's the Kimball brothers were successful contractors and builders in San Francisco. Frank's physician had told him he must move to a milder climate if he was to live more than a year, so he started down the coast, stopping in various communities trying to find the "ideal place" in which to settle.

When he reached San Diego, Kimball visited an old friend, Gen. H. S. Burton, who lived near Jamul.

He borrowed a horse and rode day after day, looking over the surrounding country. When he saw Rancho de la Nación he knew he had found his "ideal place." June 18, 1868, the Kimball brothers signed a contract to purchase the rancho from Pioche for $30,000.

The Kimballs, with Frank taking the leading role although he was the youngest of the three, saw tremendous possibilities in the rancho for development. They surveyed and cleared land, constructed roads and built a wharf on San Diego Bay. Homesites and small ranchos sold fast; many believed the new city, which they called National City, would rival, and perhaps even exceed, San Diego in population and industrial importance.

The future indeed seemed rosy for the Kimballs and their new city, but there were many disappointments in store for them. In 1869 Frank Kimball made a bid to the Memphis & El Paso Railroad Co. of 500 blocks of land if the railroad would come to San Diego Bay and a further bid of 500 blocks for a terminus in National City. San Diego also offered a large amount of land to the company. The deal fell through because the railroad could not finance the line to the west coast.

Then came the Texas Pacific Railroad with a plan to run a line to the coast. The Kimballs gave bond to convey thousands of acres of their land to the company if the line would terminate in National City.

It was about this time that Frank Kimball began to have financial troubles. He had plenty of land but little cash. A payment on the rancho was due to Pioche and it became necessary for him to sell property he owned in Oakland. He made the final payment in 1871.

The following year, in June, the first stake was driven at a spot on National Avenue on the survey of the Texas Pacific. The route across the mountains still had not been decided but Kimball had been assured that National City would be the terminus, and foundry and work shops would be there.

Then came the financial crash of 1873 and the Kimball hopes for a rail terminus were dashed again.

The two-story Brewster home was one of the finest constructed in the early days of Paradise Valley, on lands of Rancho de la Nación. The big rancho was subdivided in 1868 by Frank Kimball and his two brothers.

For the next few years Kimball devoted himself to improving the rancho. He raised sheep, and planted thousands of citrus and olive trees.

The Pacific & Atlantic Railroad, which was building its line from St. Louis across Oklahoma Territory, was having financial troubles; a merger was negotiated with the Santa Fe, and the latter threw its resources into the struggle to push the rails on into California, through the Cajon Pass and to Los Angeles.

Frank Kimball was sent to Boston, where he conferred with both Pacific & Atlantic and Santa Fe officials. The two firms and their banking interests finally agreed to form a new company and run a line from San Diego to Barstow, where it would connect with the Santa Fe. The new line was to be called the California Southern, and Kimball was assured that National City would be the terminus.

The long fight was over but the price National City and San Diego were pledged to pay was high, as Richard F. Pourade pointed out in his book, *The Glory Years*. Kimball had pledged 10,000 acres—

this was to be placed with a syndicate to be controlled by the railroad. In addition, he would sell to the syndicate additional land worth $100,000.

The Santa Fe received, from National City and San Diego, a total of 17,000 acres of land, including rights of way and waterfront privileges, and 485 lots and $25,000.

In 1881 construction of the railroad shops in National City was begun. Kimball was a director of the new railroad but he had no direct authority over the building crews. He complained bitterly to friends about inefficiency and poor management, and how relatives and friends of top officials were being placed in technical jobs for which they had no experience.

But despite setbacks, construction of the shops progressed and the rail line was pushed northward mile after mile. When it reached Colton another problem beset the California Southern—the Southern Pacific refused permission to cross its tracks and right-of-way. There was a court fight, which the California Southern won, and work was resumed.

Then came the stormy winter of 1883-84 and still another setback for the California Southern. Floodwaters washed out several miles of rails in Temecula Canyon where engineers had built the tracks as close to the bed of the stream as possible, against the advice of area residents. It was nearly a year before traffic was resumed. A new route was chosen, however, the road going north through Oceanside to San Juan Capistrano.

In 1885 the California Southern was merged with the Santa Fe and soon thereafter the machine shops were moved from National City to San Bernardino and the superintendent's office to Los Angeles.

This was a terrific blow to Frank Kimball, but he continued with his plans for development of National City and Chula Vista. The San Diego Land & Town Co., a syndicate controlled by the Santa Fe, began construction of Sweetwater Dam at the site selected by Frank Kimball. The syndicate also formed the National City & Otay Railroad Co., running a main line from Fifth and L streets, San Diego, to National City, Chula Vista and Oneonta, with branch lines to La Presa, Sweetwater Dam and Tia Juana. The latter name had not yet been changed to Tijuana.

Chula Vista was not incorporated until 1911; the

Aerial view of National City in 1968, with part of the Navy's mothball fleet in the foreground. The city was constructed on Rancho de la Nación land. Frank Kimball, who developed the city, built the first wharf.

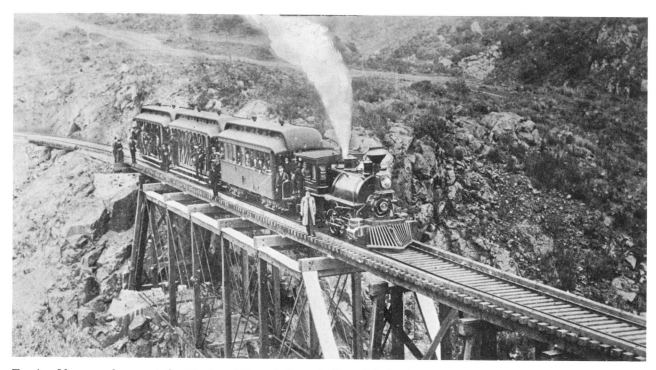

Engine No. 5 and cars of the National City & Otay Railroad halted on High Bridge, near Sweetwater Dam, for this 1888 photograph. Line connected San Diego to National City, Chula Vista, Oneonta and Tia Juana.

population then was about 3,000. Development had started, however, as early as 1888, when W. G. Dickinson, business manager of the Land & Town Co., began the subdividing of 5,000 acres. Chula Vista eventually became a suburban city of beautiful homes and growing industries.

Who is responsible for giving Chula Vista its euphonious name is uncertain; many think Dickinson chose it. "Chula" means "pretty" in Spanish. "Vista" means "view."

The development of National City came first—it was incorporated in 1887—but its population in 1968 was estimated at only 40,000, far less than that of its sister city, which was about 64,000.

Frank Kimball, who often has been called the "father" of both National City and Chula Vista, died in 1913. He had lived on Rancho de la Nación forty-five years and most of that time was in ill health. He fought hard to develop his beloved rancho and he lived to see his dreams well on the way to reality.

23

Península de San Diego Rancho

When Don Pedro C. Carrillo asked Gov. Pío Pico for a grant of 4,185 acres of brush and sand dunes across the bay from the little town of San Diego in 1846, many of his friends thought he must be out of his mind.

It would be difficult to find a less likely spot for cattle grazing than Península de San Diego Rancho. Grass was sparse, there was little water, and the only way to get cattle to or from the rancho was to drive them along the narrow strip of sand holding back the ocean from San Diego Bay.

Don Pedro of course had no way of knowing that his rancho would become the site of a thriving city, Coronado, and a mighty government military base, the U. S. Naval Air Station at North Island. Had he known he would not have sold his two "islands" for $1,000.

Young Carrillo was the son of Don Carlos Antonio Carrillo, who was *receptor*, or collector of customs, for the port of San Diego. Don Pedro was educated in Honolulu and Boston and had served a term as *alcalde* of San Diego. His wife, Doña Josefa, was the daughter of one of San Diego's most prominent citizens, Juan Bandini. Leo Carrillo, the movie actor, who died in 1961, traced his ancestry back to Don Pedro.

There was some question about the legality of the land grant, as the peninsula had been included in the boundaries of the pueblo as drawn by Capt. Henry Fitch the previous year. Fitch had been given the assignment of mapping city lands by the subprefect, Santiago Arguello. This map was ignored by the governor in making the grant. Later, when an American survey was made, the peninsula was excluded from pueblo lands and the title upheld.

Three years of trying to raise cattle on the barren acres was enough for Don Pedro; he sold Península de San Diego Rancho to Capt. Bezer Simmons, master of the American ship *Magnolia*, for $1,000 in silver.

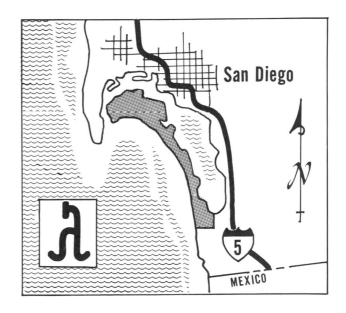

Two months later Simmons sold a one-sixteenth interest in the property to A. C. Peachy of Vermont, and Frederick Billings, who later became president of the Northern Pacific Railroad. The following year Simmons sold another small interest to William H. Aspinwall for $10,000. Col. George W. Grannis obtained title to the entire property in 1877 through a mortgage foreclosure, for $116,377.

Elisha S. Babcock, an Indiana railroad financier, came to San Diego in 1884 for his health. With him was his friend, H. L. Story of Chicago, a piano manufacturer.

Frederick Billings, a part owner of Peninsula de San Diego Rancho in 1849, filed this map with his claim.

The two often crossed the bay in a rowboat to hunt rabbits on the peninsula. One day, after tramping across to the ocean side, Babcock remarked that "this would be a wonderful spot for a resort hotel, a big one that would attract people from all over the world . . . We could buy the entire peninsula, lay out a city—sale of the lots would pay for the hotel."

Story agreed, and the two lost little time in forming a syndicate, the Coronado Beach Co. Besides Babcock and Story, the incorporators included Jacob Gruendike, San Diego banker, Joseph Collett of Terra Haute, Indiana, and Heber Ingle of Evansville, Indiana.

The peninsula was purchased for $110,000 and the new firm immediately started clearing the land. Scores of men were hired to cut and burn the brush. Grading of streets and platting of town lots followed quickly.

Babcock, president of the syndicate, wasted no time in getting started on his dream of building the finest hotel in the West. He sent for two architect friends, James W. Reid, and his brother, Merritt, in Evansville.

Babcock's instructions to James Reid were brief:

He wanted the finest hotel possible, built around a large court, the court to be a veritable garden; balconies should look down on the courtyard from every story. On the ocean corner there should be a pavilion tower.

Reid made hurried preliminary sketches for the prospectus Babcock wanted for use in selling his Coronado lots. He was in such a rush to start construction that these drawings were used in estimating building materials needed. Lumber was shipped from San Francisco, where the entire production of a redwood plant was contracted for months.

Labor also was a problem. Few experienced carpenters were available, and even common laborers were difficult to obtain. Babcock hired several hundred Chinese in San Francisco as laborers, while Reid and his few experienced carpenters undertook "on-the-job" training of all the men they could hire in San Diego.

Reid supervised the entire construction, and Hotel del Coronado became a monument to his brilliance as an architect and skill as a builder. Not only did he fulfill Babcock's dream of having the finest hotel in the West, but spurred by the promoter's haste, the 400-room structure was opened for business February 19, 1888, just eleven months from the date construction was started.

Meantime, sale of lots in Coronado was booming. The first ferry consisted of two flat boats towed by Story's little steam yacht, the *Della*. This was soon replaced by a ferryboat, the *Coronado*, built in San Francisco.

Water was a problem at first. Wells were dug in the dry bed of San Diego River near Old Town and piped across the bay. Later, water was piped from springs near the mouth of Otay River.

The Coronado Railroad Co. was organized in 1886 and a road from the bay to the ocean on Orange Avenue was completed in July of that year. Horse cars were used until a motor could be obtained.

The financial crash of 1888 hit Babcock hard. He had other financial interests in the county besides Coronado. He was one of a group that controlled the Otay and Janal ranchos and Otay Lake. He also owned the Western Salt Co. at the south end of San

Early-day photo taken from Point Loma shows entrance to San Diego Bay, undeveloped North Island, the city of Coronado and part of the Silver Strand. At high tide, North Island at that time was in reality an island.

Diego Bay and was one of the owners of the San Diego Street Car Co.

It was then that John D. Spreckels and his brother, Adolph, arrived in San Diego on the former's yacht, the *Lurline*. They were immediately entranced by San Diego and Coronado. One of the first things they did was to lend Babcock $100,000, which later he could not repay.

The investments John D. Spreckels and his brother made here did much to help the area through the depression and later.

Spreckels purchased Hotel del Coronado in 1903, together with hundreds of unsold Coronado city lots. North Island, which had never been developed, was included in the sale, as well as the Silver Strand. The island was overrun by jackrabbits and a popular sport of hotel guests was to hunt them from horseback.

Through the years, Hotel del Coronado changed little in outward appearance. There were only five owners before 1968—the Babcock syndicate, John D. Spreckels, the Barney Goodman hotel chain of Kansas City, John Alessio, and the H. D. C. Com-

pany, of which M. Larry Lawrence was president and Carleton Lichty executive vice president.

Spreckels constructed coal docks on San Diego Bay. He took over the street railway system and ferry company and purchased two daily newspapers, *The San Diego Union* and *Evening Tribune*. Later, he built the railroad connecting San Diego and Yuma, the Spreckels Theater, the Bank of America Building and the Union Building, later the Land Title Building, and developed Mission Beach.

Coronado Tent City was constructed about 1900 and was a popular resort for many years. Free band concerts and vaudeville were provided for visitors and there was ocean and bay swimming and boating.

Spreckels visualized a bay bridge about the year 1915 and employed a consulting engineer, John L. Harrington, to draw the plans. It was proposed to follow approximately the line of the ferry crossing, but the plan was given up.

The dream of a bay bridge was not realized until 1968, when work was begun on a span costing $47,-600,000.

After Spreckels died in 1926 his entire empire began to disintegrate, and with the death of his son, Claus, in 1935 most of his holdings were sold.

In 1893, eighteen acres at the southwest tip of North Island were condemned by the government for construction of a jetty to keep the San Diego Bay channel open. In 1901, an additional thirty-eight acres adjacent to the jetty were condemned to establish a coast defense fort, Pío Pico, as a substation of Fort Rosecrans. Fort Pío Pico fell into the bay during dredging operations in 1941.

North Island, now the site of the U. S. Naval Air Station, was first used as a military flying school in 1911 by Glenn L. Curtiss. It was from here that he made the first successful hydro-aeroplane flight in the United States.

Later in the same year Lieut. Theodore G. Ellyson, the first Navy officer to undergo flight training, reported to the Curtiss school. At that time North Island was separated from Coronado by a strip of shallow water a mile long and 200 yards wide called Spanish Bight.

Between January 15 and April 24, 1912, the entire flying Navy of the United States—three airplanes—was stationed at North Island. In 1913 the Army Signal Corps transferred all its aviation equipment and personnel to the island. The Coronado Beach Co. had granted permission to use the land at no cost, provided it would be relinquished on demand. The installation later was named Rockwell Field.

The 4th Marine Regiment commanded by Col. Joseph H. Pendleton established a camp on the island in 1914. He became a major general later, and Camp Pendleton Marine Corps Base was named in his honor. The island camp was abandoned in December, 1914, when the regiment was assigned to duty at the Panama-California Exposition in Balboa Park

Peninsula de San Diego Rancho was 4,185 acres of sand and brushy land across the bay from San Diego. It sold for one thousand dollars. In 1968 it contained the city of Coronado and the U.S. Naval Air Station.

and the Panama-Pacific Exposition in San Francisco. Four companies were stationed in San Diego.

In 1917, joint use of North Island was agreed on by the Army and Navy. Lieut. Earl W. Spencer was the first commanding officer of the Naval Air Station. In 1935 Rockwell Field was closed and the Navy took over the entire island.

The government had foreseen the necessity of obtaining ownership of North Island and in 1917 had instituted condemnation proceedings. In 1921, the U. S. Supreme Court awarded Spreckels $5,000,-000 for the land, plus $1,098,333 in accrued interest.

Many famous aviation "firsts" took place from North Island. Among them were:

May 3, 1923—First non-stop coast-to-coast flight. Army Lieuts. Oakley G. Kelly and John A. Mc-Cready flew 2,780 miles from New York to North Island in twenty-six hours, fifty minutes.

June 27, 1923—Army Lieuts. F. W. Seifert (later colonel) of San Diego, Virgil Hine, L. H. Smith and J. P. Richter conducted first complete mid-air pipeline refueling between two planes.

April 9, 1925—First night landing aboard a carrier made by Navy Lieut. John D. Price at sea off North Island.

May 10, 1927—Charles A. Lindbergh took off from North Island on the first leg of his flight to Paris.

December 12, 1947—First transcontinental ferry flight of a helicopter was completed at North Island by Navy Capt. C. C. Marsh.

In 1968 the Naval Air Station had a population which fluctuated between 20,000 and 30,000 persons, depending upon how many ships were tied up there. It was the largest aviation center on the West Coast.

Península de San Diego Rancho of 1846 bore little resemblance to the area of later days. Don Pedro Carrillo, could he have seen the vast developments, might have recognized the strand, although it had been widened in many places, but he surely would have seen no similarity between his brush-covered acres and the beautiful city of Coronado, and the military might represented by North Island and the Navy amphibious base on the strand.

24

Monserrate Rancho

A lonely old adobe ranchhouse atop a slight rise just a few yards from the south bank of the San Luis Rey River was in plain sight of the scores of motorists who passed by each day on Highway 395. It was the year 1968.

Its windows had been broken by vandals, doors were missing or hung from a single hinge, smashed bottles littered the floor. Outside, weeds grew thick in the patio and around the ancient house.

But the massive three-foot walls of the century-old ranchhouse still stood proudly as a reminder of olden days, when the children of Don Tomás Alvarado played in the patio or in the nine rooms of the U-shaped home, or among the barns and corrals just east of the house.

Thousands of cattle and horses once grazed the 13,322 unfenced acres of Monserrate Rancho, herded by Mexican and Indian *vaqueros*. Many servants cared for the house, did the cooking and washing and tended the vegetable garden.

Monserrate Rancho was granted to Don Ysidro María Alvarado by Gov. Pío Pico in 1846, in the closing days of Mexican rule in California. Don Ysidro built a small adobe ranchhouse on the north side of the San Luis Rey River, where he lived simply with his family, raising a few cattle and horses.

In 1862-63 a smallpox epidemic swept the area,

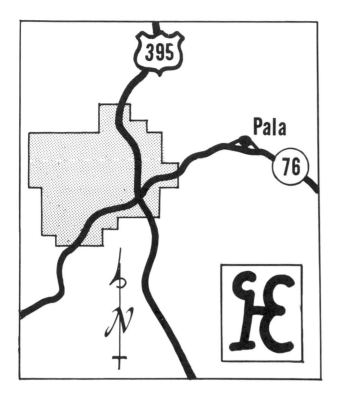

Monserrate Rancho supposedly was named after an ancient Spanish monastery. Old records differ as to the spelling; modern-day residents usually pronounce the name as Monserrat, with the accent on the last syllable.

Don Ysidro had not been too successful as a ranchero. In 1860 his land was appraised at $3,000; his personal property was valued at $7,000 and included 180 steers, twenty cows, 100 sheep and fifty horses.

His son Tomás proved to be a better business man and a few years after the father's death his herds had grown to number 3,000 cattle, 13,000 sheep and 300 horses.

As Don Tomás prospered he acquired more expensive tastes. His daughters were sent away to school and he and his wife spent large sums on furnishing their adobe home. They also entertained extensively and spent considerable time in travel.

Through the years Monserrate Rancho was broken up into many parcels of land, and cattle grazing was largely given up in favor of general farming. Many acres were devoted to dairying and commercial flower raising, and there were a number of citrus and avocado groves of various sizes.

In the late 1870's, Henry H. Gird, who had owned La Ciénaga Rancho in Los Angeles County, purchased 5,500 acres of Monserrate Rancho from one of the Alvarado daughters. His son, Will E., bought an additional 4,500 acres from another of the heirs and the two raised cattle and horses.

Henry Gird built a frame house in 1878 on what later became Gird Road; in 1914 the family constructed a 4,000-square-foot poured concrete home, some of the walls of which were fifteen inches thick.

Most of the acreage was sold during the years, and in 1946, Mrs. Nina Allen Gird of Pacific Beach, widow of Will Gird, sold the remainder, about 1,500 acres, to R. P. M. Davis & Everett of Los Angeles. This firm operated the ranch primarily for row-crops.

In 1954, Douglas Rancho, a subsidiary of the Penobscot Building, Inc., of Detroit, bought the property; cattle and row-crops were raised for many years. Later, all ranching activities ceased and two

taking the lives of many Indians and some members of the rancheros' families. By February, 1863, the dread disease had killed more than a dozen of the Monserrate Rancho *vaqueros* and servants. Don Ysidro and his wife, who had helped care for those stricken, finally contracted the disease and died also.

Their son, Don Tomás, inherited the property and built the ranchhouse on the south side of the river. Devout Catholics, Don Tomás and his wife, the former María Ignacia Moreno, constructed an adobe chapel close to the ranchhouse; walls of the small structure were still standing in 1968 although the roof had caved in. No trace remained of the adobe where Don Ysidro lived.

Don Tomás and his wife became the parents of five girls and one boy. The story is told that Doña María, before the birth of each child, would send a *vaquero* to San Gabriel Mission to get for her a small orange tree, which she would plant in the yard just outside her patio. Only one of these trees, although stunted from lack of care, survived. Imbedded in its branches was a rusty horseshoe.

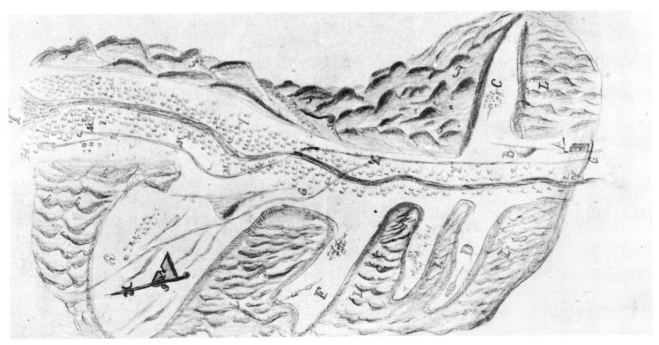

Don Ysidro María Alvarado presented this diseño *in support of his claim for lands of Monserrate Rancho. He had been granted the large tract by Gov. Pío Pico in 1846, as the Mexican rule of California neared an end.*

Sketch of the ranchhouse of Don Ysidro María Alvarado on the Monserrate Rancho. The adobe house was built on the north side of San Luis Rey River about 1846. Don Ysidro and his wife died in a smallpox epidemic.

Don Tomás Alvarado inherited Monserrate Rancho from his father and built this U-shaped adobe house on the south side of the San Luis Rey River. In 1968 the house had been abandoned and weeds filled the patio.

parcels of the land were sold. The remaining 1,285 acres were held for future development.

Edgar S. Dulin in 1968 had the largest single parcel of land, 2,000 acres, remaining of the Monserrate grant. He farmed 850 acres, and also had avocado, lemon and orange groves. About 200 acres were leased for the growing of gladiolus bulbs. Dulin grazed a small herd of Hereford cattle on the remaining acreage.

Many arrowheads and other Indian relics were found on the ranch. An old Indian deer trap was discovered many years ago in a canyon on the cattle range. Long brush-woven fence-wings led the deer to an opening between two large rocks, beyond which was a corral made of tightly woven branches.

Rancho Viejo was a 600-acre dairy ranch that was part of the Monserrate grant. Owned by Myron Guilbert and Dr. Irvin L. Watkins, the rancho was leased to Mr. and Mrs. F. H. (Bucky) Harris.

Douglas Shearer, Hollywood movie director, purchased about 700 acres of the Monserrate grant. Rancho Viejo was part of the property. Shearer later sold the dairy to Guilbert and Watkins.

The remaining 100 acres, across Highway 395 from the dairy, was the site of the old Alvarado ranchhouse. Shearer restored the adobe, but as no one occupied the house it soon began to deteriorate and vandals contributed to its state of disrepair. Gordon Kaylor of Fallbrook later purchased the property.

Within the original boundaries of the grant also was a large residential development called Pala Mesa, and the Pala Mesa Golf Club, Inn and Lodge.

Well-kept grounds of the Pala Mesa Golf Club replaced many acres of grazing land on Monserrate Rancho. A housing development, stores, and ranches ranging in size to 2,000 acres also were on rancho lands in 1968.

25

San Felipe Rancho

San Felipe Rancho, in the days when the Mexican Dons ruled vast tracts of ranch land in Southern California, was known as the desert gateway to San Diego.

It is still one of two gateways from Imperial Valley, being situated at the foot of Banner Grade at Scissors Crossing, and also on the road to Warner Hot Springs.

The rolling hills and grassy valleys where once Mexican *vaqueros* herded thousands of cattle and horses have changed little in the last century. But the rangy, horned cattle that were valuable mostly for their hides gave way in time to sleek, chunky Herefords.

Indian rancherías dotted the fertile San Felipe Valley, named for Saint Philip, when the Spanish explorer, Pedro Fages, camped there in 1782 en route to San Diego from Sonora. He is supposed to have named the valley.

Other explorers, adventurers and missionaries followed this route from Yuma to San Diego, and when the Butterfield Stage Line began operating in 1858 from Missouri to San Francisco, a stage station was constructed on the San Felipe Rancho near what later became Scissors Crossing on Highway 78. There teams were changed before the hard pull up the mountain to Warner Ranch. The station also was used by the military during the Civil War.

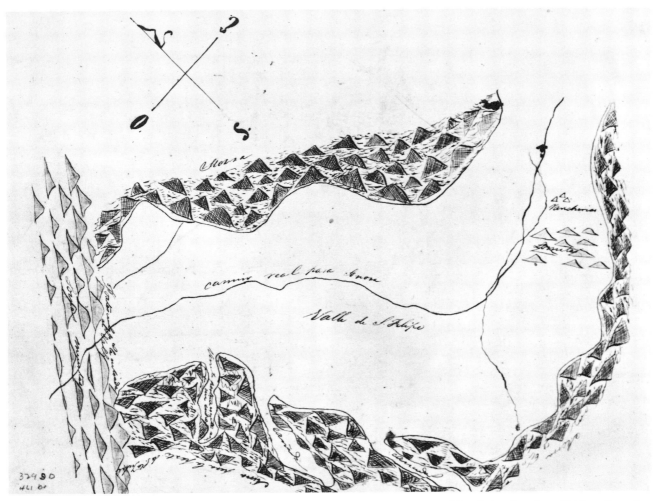

Juan Forster submitted this diseño *before the U.S. Land Commission in his claim for San Felipe Rancho. Felipe Castillo, an Indian, was the first owner of the property, and received title from Gov. Pío Pico in 1846.*

The first legal owner of the rancho was an Indian, Felipe Castillo, to whom the 9.972-acre tract was granted in 1846 by Pío Pico, the last Mexican governor of California.

History is vague about the identity of Castillo. Some writers even have hinted that this was a fictitious name.

Soon the property was transferred to Don Juan Forster, owner of Rancho de la Nación and who later purchased Rancho Santa Margarita y las Flores.

The night of December 1, 1846, Gen. Stephen W. Kearny's troops camped at San Felipe Rancho on their way to San Diego. The next day they continued to Warner Ranch.

A few days later the American detachment was attacked by a force of Californios at San Pasqual.

The following month the Mormon Battalion came through the rancho on its historic trek to open a military wagon road from Council Bluffs, Iowa, to San Diego.

The next owners of the rancho were Francois Louis Pioche and J. B. Bayerque, who also purchased Rancho de la Nación from Forster. About 1900, the property was bought by Thomas L. Duque, who constructed the large, two-story adobe-and-wood ranchhouse which in 1968 was still in excellent condition.

George Sawday, pioneer San Diego County cat-

Barren hills surround the semi-desert range lands of San Felipe Rancho. Pedro Fages, the Spanish explorer, made camp here in 1782. A Butterfield Stage station was established in the south end of the valley about 1858.

tleman, leased San Felipe during many years of the Duque ownership, and after Duque's death, purchased the rancho from the heirs. After Sawday's death, his widow, Mrs. Emily Sawday, became owner. Her son-in-law, Orville A. Cumming, operated the rancho and other Sawday ranch properties.

As the result of a property division, Hans Starr, also a son-in-law of Mrs. Sawday, operated the northern half of the ranch in partnership with Edward Rutherford of Imperial Valley, under the name Starr-Rutherford Cattle Co. This range adjoined the firm's 12,000-acre Volcan Ranch in the Julian area.

No trace remained in 1968 of any ranchhouse built before the Duque structure.

Modern operation of the rancho in the 1960's was a far cry from the methods used by Don Juan

Forster a century ago. Then the cattle and horses were allowed to roam the thousands of unfenced acres. Roundups were conducted in the spring, when the animals were branded. Most of the cattle were sold for their hides; some were trail-herded to San Diego.

The *vaqueros* were hard-riding Mexicans and Indians. Branding was done on the range. Calves were roped and dragged to a fire, where a *vaquero* applied a hot iron to the animal's hip or ribs. There was no thought of range conservation nor up-grading of cattle.

The modern ranchero usually brands his cattle in a chute and does not mark his horses. And the wild, scrawny steers of the Days of the Dons have been replaced by placid, slow-moving, chunky animals a hundred times more valuable than their forebears.

106

26

Rancho de la Misión San Diego de Alcalá

When Father Junípero Serra brought Christianity to California in 1769 and constructed the first mission on Presidio Hill, he also became the state's first agriculturalist and cattle rancher.

Under the Franciscan padre's direction huge tracts of land in San Diego County were taken over by the Catholic Church in trust for the Indians. It was Father Serra's hope that, with their conversion to Christianity and the education he would give them, the Indians eventually could become self-supporting and able to work the farms and ranchos.

The good padre's hopes were never realized. Hundreds of the natives were converted, and many labored faithfully in the fields under the direction of the Franciscan fathers. But the natural antipathy of these Indians for work, together with the greed and aggressiveness of the white residents of this new land, conspired to defeat the plans of Father Serra and the padres who labored with him.

The Indians here were not as warlike as those of the Plains tribes, although there were many instances of attacks on ranchos. Even the mission, San Diego de Alcalá, newly built in Mission Valley, was attacked and partly burned in 1775. One of the padres, Father Luis Jayme, was killed in the attack,

to become the first Christian martyr in California.

The padres operated a school for the Indians in addition to their church duties, and managed the affairs of their farms and vineyards, and supervised their herds and flocks. Outlying ranchos operated by the padres before secularization of all the California missions in 1834 included El Cajón, Santa María, San José del Valle, Santa Margarita, San Bernardo, Los Coches, El Rincón del Diablo, and Santa Ysabel.

In addition, the church's Rancho de la Misión San Diego de Alcalá, with 58,875 acres, extended from the boundary of the pueblo of San Diego inland to El Cajon Valley, and from National City to Clairemont. Included were what later became Linda Vista, part of the Miramar Naval Air Station, Allied Gardens, Kensington, East San Diego, San Diego State College, La Mesa, Encanto and Lemon Grove. This rancho was retained after the secularization act became effective.

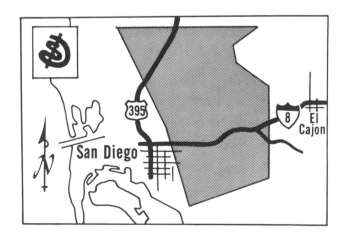

A report on the mission, requested by the government in 1827, shows the padres' success in building up Church holdings. They listed acreage devoted to growing wheat, corn and beans, as well as large vineyards and olive groves.

The following livestock totals were given: Cattle, 9,120; sheep, 16,284; tame horses, 169; mules, 825; goats, 234, and swine, 72.

Droughts in 1801 and 1803 caused the mission fathers to decide to construct a dam across Mission

Misión San Diego de Alcalá as it looked about 1899. Following secularization of the California missions and seizure of all church properties by the Mexican authorities, the buildings were neglected and fell into ruins.

Gorge about three miles east of the church. Fathers Fernando Martín and José Sánchez were in charge of the work, with mission Indians as the laborers. An aqueduct constructed of tiles, resting on stones set in cement, carried a stream a foot deep and two feet wide from the dam, which was 220 feet long and thirteen feet thick at its base, through the gorge to the mission. Traces of the dam and aqueduct remained more than a century later, attesting to the engineering skill of the padres.

Father Martín died in 1838, at the age of sixty-eight. His remains lay beneath the floor of the present restored mission church in 1968.

The Mexican government decree of August 9, 1834, ordered confiscation of all the missions and their properties. The padres, who had done their best through the years to hold the lands for the Indians, quietly submitted to the inevitable.

On September 20, Misión San Diego de Alcalá was transferred officially from Father Martín to José Rocha, who had been appointed commissioner for that purpose. The inventory included everything, and church goods and sacred vessels were not excepted.

In April of 1835, Joaquín Ortega was made administrator at a salary of fifty dollars a month, to be paid from income of church property. The church and its appurtenances were valued at $4,777.37. Debts were listed as $531, but the military still owed the mission $18,816.75 for supplies.

On May 17, 1841, Father Vicente Pasqual Oliva wrote to the governor's secretary that the mission had become so poor after six years of administrator rule that there was not enough produce on hand to pay the annual salary of $140 to the *mayordomo*, Juan Osuna.

The final blow to the mission came in 1845 when Pío Pico, the last Mexican governor, decreed that Rancho Misión San Diego de Alcalá be turned over to Don Santiago Arguello "in consideration of past services to the territorial government." The deed was drafted June 8, 1846, in Los Angeles. Under its terms Arguello was to pay the mission's debts, support the priests and maintain religious services.

Don Santiago had been prominent in San Diego affairs and had held several political and military offices. He was *comandante* of the Presidio from 1827 to 1835. He was granted the Ti Juan Rancho, now the city of Tijuana, in 1829. During the conquest by the United States he was captain of a troop of the California Battalion. He died in 1862.

Arguello's heirs received a patent to the rancho in 1876 and the lands were opened to settlement in 1885.

In 1847, the Mormon Battalion under Lieut. Col. Philip Cook was stationed at the mission for a short time. In 1848, troops under Maj. Samuel P. Heintzelman were stationed there, and soldiers remained

on duty at the mission until 1859, when they were moved to the barracks at New San Diego.

Also in 1848, the ex-Mission Rancho was leased by Philip Crosthwaite, a San Diego business man and former sheriff. At one time he owned the two square blocks bounded by Fifth, Fourth, C and E streets in San Diego.

Crosthwaite lost several hundred cattle during a drought, then traded his lease on the mission lands for a lease on Rancho La Misión in Baja California. He later purchased this rancho, on which there was a large spring, water from which later was piped about thirty-five miles to Tijuana.

Crosthwaite had eight sons and three daughters, and as late as 1968 many of their descendants lived in San Diego or Baja California. Among these were three great grandsons, Francis G., Frederick N., and Rupert J. Crosthwaite. By a strange coincidence, each of the three brothers resided within the area their great grandfather leased from Don Santiago Arguello. Their father owned the Baja California rancho, but he was killed in an auto accident in

Sketch shows the home and citrus grove of Will M. Smith in Chollas Valley, on land of Rancho de la Misión San Diego de Alcalá. The rancho was removed from church control and given to Santiago Arguello in 1846.

Excavations made by the University of San Diego on the grounds of Misión San Diego de Alcalá in 1968 uncovered the foundations of a long adobe building where sabers, a saw, spurs and other objects were found.

1927. Most of the cattle and horses were stolen by rustlers and Mrs. Crosthwaite finally lost the land when it was overrun by squatters.

Following the secularization of the missions and the hard times it brought for the padres, the authority of the church began to diminish, the Indian converts drifted away and returned to their old way of life, and the mission buildings fell into disrepair. With the loss of Rancho de la Misión the padres were practically destitute.

The missions were to become parish churches. and the padres disappeared from the California scene. Many years later, on May 23, 1862, a decree by President Abraham Lincoln returned twenty-two and one-fifth acres to the church.

The mission church and adjoining buildings were largely restored, although improvement work continued for many years.

Directly behind the long, low building adjoining the church, excavations were conducted in 1968 by the archaeology class of the University of San Diego. The baked adobe tile floors of the original structure. where the padres lived, were uncovered, and also parts of the adobe walls, still showing the plaster which had been applied both inside and outside.

The excavations also uncovered three sabers. each about three and one-half feet long, a seven-foot saw blade. a balance scales and grinding wheel, as well as horseshoes. metal buckles. stirrups and spurs, and broken bottles.

Father Serra and the padres who succeeded him played an important role in early development of San Diego County and its ranch lands. The Indian converts were many and their descendants lived on the many Indian reservations in San Diego's backcountry in later years. most of them retaining the Catholic faith of their forefathers.

The padres failed in their long fight to conserve the valuable ranch lands for their converts. but they left an indelible imprint on the history of San Diego County.

Language of the Ranchos

San Dieguito Rancho

—OSUNA

Monserrate Rancho

—ALVARADO

Pauma Rancho

—SERRANO

Península de San Diego Rancho

—CARRILLO

Otay Rancho

—ESTUDILLO

El Cajón Rancho

—PEDRORENA

Cuyamaca Rancho

—OLVERA

Rancho Santa Margarita

—PICO

Jamul Rancho

—PICO

Agua Hedionda Rancho

—MARRON

Brand Meanings Are Lost

The Mexican "picture" brands used by many of the Dons to mark their cattle and horses more than a century ago are puzzling to present-day cattlemen.

"They don't make any sense," said one rancher. "They're just a lot of straight and curved lines—and many of the lines were so close together they'd blot."

"Those brands look odd to us now," said another cattleman, "but I'm sure each one meant something."

The San Dieguito Rancho brand of Don Juan María Osuna was one of the "picture" type. Don Juan's great grandson, Ramón Osuna, who was born on the rancho in 1882, could not explain the meaning of his ancestor's brand.

"I never saw my grandfather or great-grandfather," he said. "I don't know if my father, Julio, knew the meaning or not; anyway, he had discarded the old Osuna brand and used his initials, but the letters were reversed, making his brand O-J."

Modern-day brands are as simple as possible, like the Box D, Flying W, Anchor and L5, all easily described and readily identified. In the Days of the Dons a "picture" brand was referred to as belonging to Monserrate Rancho, the Serrano family, or the Carrillos, but it had no distinctive name.

The anchor-like brand of Otay Rancho, still in use in 1968, is said to include all the letters of the name Estudillo. Some modern ranchers find this difficult to believe. A few of the Dons used clearly defined initials, such as MP (together), Miguel de Pedrorena, and AO (together), Agustín Olvera.

In stocking a new rancho, a brand was sometimes purchased with a herd of cattle. Presumably this was the case when the Pico brothers, Pío and Andrés, were granted Rancho Santa Margarita. Their brand was a T atop an O.

Many families had several brands and this custom continues today. Different markings were registered for sons and daughters.

J. C. La Force, a cattleman who long studied ranch history and who collected hundreds of old branding irons, spurs, bits, Mexican saddles and other equipment used by the rancheros, said each of the "picture" brands had a meaning, although perhaps known only to its owner.

"If you study them you can come up with a lot of possibilities," he said. "The Jamul brand, for instance, might be the face of a steer, with the curved line above forming its horns. And the Agua Hedionda brand could be interpreted as a walking man."

C. L. Hubbard of the Bureau of Livestock Identification, Sacramento, agreed with La Force. "It is unfortunate that the meanings of these brands have been lost with the passing of the rancho founders," he said. "Many of the markings had meanings known only to the users and cannot be interpreted today."

The Dons branded their stock on the left hip; when sold, the new owner placed his brand on the left shoulder. Horses were often marked on the neck with a smaller iron so the mane would cover the scar.

Modern-day ranchers brand on the hip or ribs of either side of their cattle, and sometimes on the shoulder. Seldom is a horse branded, unless the owner has a large herd on unfenced range.

The Ranchos—
What Their Names Mean
in English

Agua Hedionda—*stinking water*

Buena Vista—*good view*

Cañada de San Vicente—*glen of St. Vincent*

Cuca—*a root used as a substitute for coffee*

Cuyamaca—*rain above*

El Cajón—*the box; technically, the pass between two hills*

El Rincón del Diablo—*the devil's corner, or nook of the devil*

Guajome—*home of the frog*

Guejito y Cañada de Palomía—*small pebbles and glen of the little pigeon*

Jamacha—*wild squash vine or gourd*

Jamul—*slimy water*

Janal—*spongy ground*

La Cañada de los Coches—*the glen of the hogs*

Las Encinitas—*the little live oaks*

Los Peñasquitos—*the little cliffs*

Los Vallecitos de San Marcos—*the little valleys of St. Mark*

Misión San Diego de Alcalá—*Mission St. Didacus of Alcalá*

Monserrate—*name of a monastery in Spain*

Rancho de la Nación—*National Ranch*

Otay—*brushy*

Pauma—*I bring water*

Península de San Diego—*peninsula of San Diego*

San Bernardo—*St. Bernard*

San Dieguito—*probably little San Diego*

San Felipe—*St. Philip*

San José del Valle—*St. Joseph of the valley*

Santa Margarita y las Flores—*St. Margaret and the flowers*

Santa María—*St. Mary*

Santa Ysabel—*St. Isabel*

Valle de San José—*valley of St. Joseph*

Cities and Towns—
What Their Names Mean
in English

Agua Caliente—*hot water*

Ballena—*whale, whalebone*

Bonita—*pretty*

Campo—*field*

Chula Vista—*good view*

Coronado—*possibly named after Francisco Vásquez de Coronado, Spanish explorer*

Dehesa—*pasture or grass land*

De Luz—*of light*

Del Dios—*of God*

Del Mar—*of the sea*

Descanso—*rest or resting place*

Dulzura—*sweetness*

El Cajon—*the box*

Encanto—*enchantment, charm or delight*

Encinitas—*little live oaks*

Escondido—*secluded, hidden*

Guatay—*derived from Diegueño Indian word meaning "large"*

Jacumba—*possibly from Diegueño Indian word meaning "water"*

La Jolla—*the jewel*

La Mesa—*the plateau*

La Presa—*the dam*

La Punta—*the point or tip*

Mesa Grande—*large plateau*

Miramar—*view of the sea*

Monte Vista—*mountain view*

Morena—*possibly named after a mountain range in Spain*

Murrieta—*proper name*

Olivenhain—*olive grove*

Pala—*shovel, trowel, scoop*

Palomar—*dovecote or pigeon coop; also, string or cord made of vegetable fibre*

Potrero—*cattle ranch, stock farm*

Ramona—*named after the heroine of a novel by the same name*

Rancho Santa Fe—*Holy Faith Ranch*

San Diego—*St. Didacus*

San Luis Rey—*St. Louis, King*

Solana—*sunny place*

Tijuana—*Aunt Jane or Joanne*

Vallecito—*little valley*

Vista—*view*

In Appreciation

To the many ranchers, State Forestry officials, historical society members and descendants of the Dons for their assistance, and especially to Ramón Osuna, J. C. La Force and Cloyd Sorensen.

Reference Works

The Silver Dons and *The Glory Years* by Richard F. Pourade, *Jackrabbits to Jets* by Elretta Sudsbury, *The Coronado Story* by J. Harold Peterson, *Some Old Ranchos and Adobes* by Philip S. Rush, *The History of San Diego County Ranchos* published by Title Insurance and Trust Company, and documents from the Junípero Serra Museum, San Diego Library and National City Public Library.

Artwork Sources

Original paintings of a *Spanish Wedding Party* and *Stokes and Kearny* by Richard Gabriel Chase; watercolor sketches of early San Diego County homes by E. S. Fenyes, from Southwest Museum, Los Angeles; sketches of *diseños* presented to the Land Grant Commission, from Bancroft Library, University of California, Berkeley; illustrations of county residences from *History of San Diego County*, published by Wallace W. Elliott & Co., San Francisco, 1883; historical photographs, from Title Insurance and Trust Company; modern photographs by Ed Neil, Union-Tribune Publishing Co.; rancho maps by Bob Fassett, Union-Tribune Publishing Co.

Colophon

Printed at Anderson, Ritchie & Simon in 10 Pt. Waverly type, with Jansen and Caslon Inline display. Lithographed on 80# Natural Sonata Book. Color separations by Mission Engraving. Binding by Pacific Library Binding. Design by Joseph Simon.